INSIGHT POCKET GUIDE

&
The Gold Coast

Discovery Channel

APA PUBLICATIONS
Part of the Langenscheidt Publishing Group

Queensland
250 km / 155 miles
Badu I.
Moa I.
Torres Strait
Thursday I.
Horn I.
Prince of Wales I.
Cape York
Bamaga
JARDINE RIVER N.P.
Cape Grenville
IRON RANGE N.P.
Weipa
Cape
York
Peninsula
Coen
Gulf of
Carpentaria
Coral Sea
Great
Barrier
Reef
Princess Charlotte Bay
Cape Melville
LAKEFIELD NATIONAL PARK
Kowanyama
Laura
Cooktown
Helenvale
Lakeland Downs
DAINTREE N.P.
Mossman
PACIFIC
OCEAN
Mitchell
Mornington I.
Wellesley Is.
Bentinck I.
Port Douglas
Mareeba
Mungana
Cairns
Atherton Tableland
Atherton
Burketown
Karumba
Normanton
Ravenshoe
Innisfail
Tully
Riversleigh
Croydon
Mt Surprise
Hinchinbrook I.
Ingham
Greenvale
GREGORY RANGE
Norman
Flinders
MT SPEC N.P.
Magnetic I.
Townsville
Ayr
Camooweal
Lake Moondarra
GREAT DIVIDING RANGE
Bowen
Whitsunday Group
Charters Towers
Mount Isa
Cloncurry
Flinders Hwy
Julia Creek
Hughenden
PORCUPINE GORGE N.P.
Proserpine
Mackay
Sarina
Broad Sound
Dajarra
Kynuna
Middleton
Winton
Bruce Hwy
Muttaburra
Clermont
Boulia
Tropic of Capricorn
Yeppoon
Rock-hampton
Great Keppel I.
Barcaldine
Longreach
Emerald
Capricorn Hwy
Dingo
Diamantina
Bedourie
Gladstone
Blackall
Biloela
Barcoo
CARNAVON NATIONAL PARK
Bundaberg
GREAT SANDY N. P.
Windorah
Yaraka
Birdsville
Childers
Hervey Bay
QUEENSLAND
Augathella
Taroom
Maryborough
Fraser Island
Gympie
Charleville
Quilpie
Mitchell
Roma
Miles
Murgon
Maroochydore
Clifton Hills
Warrego Hwy
Sunshine Coast
Darling Downs
Caboolture
SOUTH AUSTRALIA
Innamincka
Dalby
Moreton I.
Thargomindah
Toowoomba
BRISBANE
Sturt Desert
Cunnamulla
Bollon
St George
Mitchell Hwy
Goondiwindi
Hungerford
Dirranbandi
Warwick
Gold Coast
GREY RANGE
STURT N.P.
Wompah
LAMINGTON N.P.
Murwillumbah
Marree
Barringun
GAMMON RANGES N.P.
Milparinka
Wanaaring
Goodooga
Tenterfield
Gwydir Hwy
Brewarrina
Moree
Leigh Creek
Lake Frome
NEW SOUTH WALES
Collarenebri
Bourke
Walgett
Glen Innes
Lake Torrens
FLINDERS RANGES
Packsaddle
Darling
Narrabri
Grafton
MOOTWINGEE N.P.
FLINDERS RANGES N.P.
Euriowie
Coolabah
Coonamble
Coffs Harbour
Pacific Hwy
NEW ENGLAND RANGE
Hawker
Broken Hill
Wilcannia
Cobar
Nyngan
Tamworth
Barrier Hwy
Cockburn
Menindee
Gilgandra
Port Macquarie

Welcome

This guidebook combines the interests and enthusiasms of two of the world's best-known information providers: Insight Guides, who have set the standard for visual travel guides since 1970, and Discovery Channel, the world's premier source of non-fiction television programming. Its aim is to show readers the best of Brisbane and the Gold Coast in a series of tailor-made itineraries devised by Insight's correspondent in Queensland Paul Phelan.

In the past few decades, Brisbane has shed its image as Australia's biggest country town to become a proud, colourful, young city. Only 100km (62 miles) south of Brisbane lies the Gold Coast. The Coast's first foreign visitors came in search of timber and some stayed to enjoy the surf. Its present residents and visitors also enjoy hundreds of other forms of entertainment.

The first eight tours in the guide concentrate on Brisbane and its immediate surroundings, though they also include a drive up the magnificent and unspoilt Sunshine Coast north of Brisbane. As well as linking the essential sights, the tours include a whale-watching trip to Moreton Island and a dawn balloon flight over the city. Tours 9–14 concentrate on the Gold Coast and its myriad attractions, from theme parks to the sandswept wilderness of Fraser Island and the virgin rainforest of Wanggoolba Creek. The tours are supported by sections on history and culture, shopping, eating out, nightlife, a calendar of events and a detailed practical information section that includes a list of hand-picked hotels.

Paul Phelan has spent most of his life in Queensland's bush and provincial centres. He has worked as an airline pilot and has managed two of the state's remotest holiday resorts. Originally a southerner, he appreciates his adopted state's laid-back culture and the dry, indomitable humour and rugged independence of its citizens. He particularly admires its unusually strong links between city and bush.

Gold Coast Itineraries

Leisure Activities

Calendar of Events

Practical Information

Maps

Index and Credits

Preceding Pages: summer fun, Hastings Point
Following Pages: Broadwater view

MLC
MLC
Country Comfort
LENNONS HOTEL

The Petrie Tableau

History & Culture

An old English proverb declares, 'Jack's as good as his master'. Much of Australia's early settlement and development was accomplished either by emancipated convicts, by immigrants so poor that they enjoyed few advantages over their newly-freed countrymen or by soldiers and marines who had come to oversee the prisons and stayed to seek wealth in the new country. Underlying the young country's progress was the realisation that the existing social structure was not up to exploiting the opportunities presented by a newly discovered land. The powerful urge to improve the quality of life meant that the creative, the diligent and those unafraid of hard work were rewarded whatever their rank in society – and still are. Today, some visitors are astonished by the lack of subservience, the egalitarianism and the irreverence for its institutions that characterises Australian life.

Early days

European seaborne explorers knew there was a large landmass between the Indian and Pacific oceans. Early charts showed small stretches of plotted coastline, linked by dotted lines which made assumptions about the rest of Terra Australis Incognita, the unknown south land. So incomplete was the early navigators' knowledge that those charts showed Australia and the islands of Tasmania and New Guinea as a contiguous landmass. It was a trick of history that the early Dutch, French, Portuguese and Spanish navigators made their landfalls on the less hospitable coastlines of what are now South Australia, Western Australia and the Northern Territory, and continued their voyages unimpressed with the land and what they had seen.

It was Britain's good fortune that Captain James Cook's first sighting of Australia was on the far more fertile east coast, and that his voyage of exploration plotted the eastern coastline from about midway between Melbourne and Sydney in the south to Cape York, the northernmost point on the continent. The bulk of Australia's population still lives along the coastal strip between Adelaide and Cairns, because that is where the most productive land is found and where most of the rain falls.

But it wasn't the perception of rich agricultural or mining opportunities that first interested the British. Rather, it was a pressing need to reduce the teeming populations of its prisons and of the hulks moored in the Thames onto which they had overflowed when the War of Independence ended the practice of transporting convicts to America. Thus, the First Fleet that sailed into Sydney Cove on 13 May,

Left: sculpture dedicated to the Petrie family, model early settlers. **Right**: Captain Cook

1787, carried not well-equipped agricultural settlers, builders or miners, but convicts and scarlet-jacketed marines. The British government hoped that this motley first population would be the foundation stone of a colony.

Brisbane was the last major colonial port to be established. Its main role was to be a convict settlement for repeat-offence prisoners in the colony of New South Wales. The initial camp in Mi-an-jin country at Redcliffe was mosquito-ridden and lacked a decent water supply. In 1825 the colony was moved to the site of Brisbane's central business district, 20km (12 miles) up the river, which was judged to be navigable by ship. This site was selected on account of its reliable water supply, the security afforded by the bend in the river, and an upstream location which served to frustrate easy escape by sea – not factors generally considered as foundations for spatial and economic growth. The governor of Brisbane proceeded with plans for the settlement believing that 'the establishment of penal depots is the best means of paving the way for the introduction of free population'. The number of convicts reached a peak of 947 in 1831, and declined thereafter until free settlement. Governor George Bowen, finding only seven and a half pence in the treasury, noted that he was 'in the position of an autocrat; the sole source of authority here, without a single soldier or a single shilling'. He was advised by London 'never to let his thoughts stray from finance'.

The site, although lacking the consummate utility of Sydney harbour, was an adequate port. But its real advantage started to become clear with the discovery, in 1827, of rich farmland at Darling Downs to Brisbane's immediate west. The British government wasn't keen on supporting a population that promised it little or no economic return, so the new colony was expected to make itself self-sufficient, and quickly. At the same time, new convicts kept arriving, and the convict colonies were establishing their potential as the embryos of new commercial communities. Although women were not among the earliest convicts, an increasing number of female prisoners began arriving, and the Female Factory was built in the late 1820s, its inmates engaged in needlework and laundry. When the women were moved to Eagle Farm in 1837, the compound was used as a location for the annual distribution of blankets to the Aborigines on Queen Victoria's birthday. By 1888, temporary convict-built structures alongside Queen Street had been replaced by large buildings, reflecting the strength of the growing local economy.

Discovery and Development

Among the first discoveries of economic importance were the vast reserves of timber, which were put to good use in the colony's new buildings, and also exploited for export. Until 1842, a government decree had forbidden unauthorised people to approach within 80km (50 miles) of the settlement. However, at that time Britain, under pressure to discontinue convict transportation, closed the Moreton Bay penal settlement, and declared the area open to free settlers. Private

Left: Queen Victoria guards the Old Treasury

enterprise soon grasped the opportunities for economic and social growth. Brisbane's population rose from 829 in 1846 to almost 6,000 by the time Queensland became a self-governing colony in 1859.

As the British set about dismantling their colonial prisons, successive journeys of exploration began to disclose immense opportunities for rural production: sheep-grazing in the west; farming in the higher-rainfall Darling Downs; sugar (first planted at Redland Bay) on the coastal flood plains; and cattle-grazing in the tropical and subtropical savannas between the coast and the arid interior. Mining was to come later, and would bring new surges in investment, exploration, and population. Although smaller ports were established all the way up the Queensland coast, Brisbane retained its status as the capital before and after federation, and was the major centre from which settlement radiated outwards.

On top of a massive wave of land development came the gold rushes, some of them fizzling out and some sustained, bringing further spurts of population and opening up new areas of exploration as far north as Cooktown, where Captain Cook had beached his vessel for repairs in 1770. As Queensland's pastoral production came of age, significant regional centres developed along the east coast, and along inland rivers and trade routes. The booming production continued apace until the Great Depression of 1929–31, by which time Brisbane had established itself as a major commercial centre. The architecture of buildings such as Parliament House and the Queensland Club, which provided country politicians and public servants with a city base, reflect the optimism of the 1880s. This feel-good factor has been the basis of Brisbane's confidence ever since.

During World War II, Brisbane became a major base for Americans serving in the Pacific theatre, with General Douglas MacArthur directing the campaign from the eighth floor of the A.M.P. Building (now MacArthur Chambers)

Top: Parliament House
Right: early transport

in Queen Street. One early and memorable conflict was a vigorous and physical exchange of views called 'the Battle of Brisbane', between the Americans and Australian soldiers, who cited three grievances against their allies – they were 'overpaid, oversexed, and over here'. The Battle of the Coral Sea, commemorated annually in Brisbane, finally united these two individualistic and assertive groups in a spirit of comradeship.

In the years since the end of World War II, Brisbane has continued to grow in stature, aided by ever-increasing tourism and internal migration from southern states, and of coal, copper, aluminium and gold mining.

The Gold Coast

The Gold Coast's first settlers were the lumberjacks of the mid-1800s. These hardy souls felled coveted red cedars from the virgin hinterland forests, before floating the timber down the rivers on the annual floods to the tidal reaches. They then assembled the rafts which they navigated to Brisbane's sawmills, skillfully using the winds and tides.

Southport soon became a popular weekend retreat for Brisbane's citizens. In 1877 the Nerang River ferry embarked on its maiden voyage to the main surfing beach. But it took the considerable imagination of one of the coast's first entrepreneurs, James Cavill, to set the Coast on its path to fame. Building the third hotel in the area, he boldly called it Surfers' Paradise. (The region's other symbolic name was formalised in 1959, when the small centres along the strip were united by the establishment of the City of the Gold Coast.) The Nerang River ferry provided the final link, and a railway line from Brisbane was completed in time for the January 1901 inauguration of Australia's federation. The bridge that replaced the ferry in 1925 irrevocably consigned what was to become the Gold Coast to the status of a real-estate bazaar.

Top: Surfers' Paradise in the 1950s
Left: surf's up, Coolum Bay

History Highlights

50,000BC (approximately) The first Aborigines arrive, apparently displacing at least two preceding waves of population of different but unknown origin. Population (at the time of European settlement) has been estimated at 300,000, at its densest along the north and east coasts.

1770 (15 May) Captain James Cook, aboard the *Endeavour*, sails past and names Point Danger, which now marks the Queensland–New South Wales border.

1787 (13 May) Britain's First Fleet sails into Sydney Cove.

1799 Explorer and navigator Matthew Flinders, in the sloop *Norfolk*, names Red Cliffe Point, which then becomes the site of Queensland's first European settlement.

1823 Surveyor-General John Oxley locates and navigates the mouth of the (now) Brisbane River.

1824 First convicts and jailers arrive at Redcliffe, on Moreton Bay.

1825 Convict settlement moved to the present site of Brisbane's central business district.

1827 The rich pastoral country of the Darling Downs is discovered.

1831 Convict population peaks at 947.

1842 Brisbane is declared open for free settlement.

1846 The schooner *Coolangatta* wrecked off what was to become the Gold Coast. Brisbane becomes a port of entry.

1848 Queensland's first immigrant ship, the *Artemisia*, reaches Moreton Bay.

1859 Statehood comes with separation from New South Wales and the naming of Queensland (European population 23,520).

1860s Sugar planted at Redland Bay, providing a ready source of rum.

1864 A disastrous fire destroys almost the entire city block contained by George, Queen, Albert and Elizabeth streets.

1875 Cobb & Co initiates a coach service linking Brisbane with Nerang Heads.

1877 Nerang River Ferry's first voyage

1887 Brisbane connected by rail to Sydney. Difficulties (which still exist) arose because of Queensland's choice of narrow gauge which did not match that of the southern states.

1901 (1 January) Inauguration of the Australian federation. Australia's first governor, Lord Hopeton, is sworn in.

1914 The first Australian troops leave home to join the allies in World War I.

1933 The Surfers' Paradise township is named after James Cavill's hotel of the same name.

1939 Outbreak of World War II: Australian forces leave again to fight in Europe and the Middle East – later in the war, Australia's military forces fight the Japanese in the Pacific theatre.

1941 (22 December) First convoy of US servicemen arrives in Brisbane, which becomes a large military base.

1959 (16 May) The city of Gold Coast established.

1974 Cyclone Wanda crosses the coast. Brisbane's worst flood since 1893.

1982 The 12th Commonwealth Games contribute to Brisbane's latter-day coming of age.

1988 Australia's bicentenary celebrations. Brisbane hosts World Expo '88 with the Queensland-friendly theme: 'Leisure in the Age of Technology'.

1990s Brisbane's population reaches the 1.5 million mark.

2000 onwards In a drive to enhance its status as a major tourist destination, Brisbane improves its attractions and infrastructure.

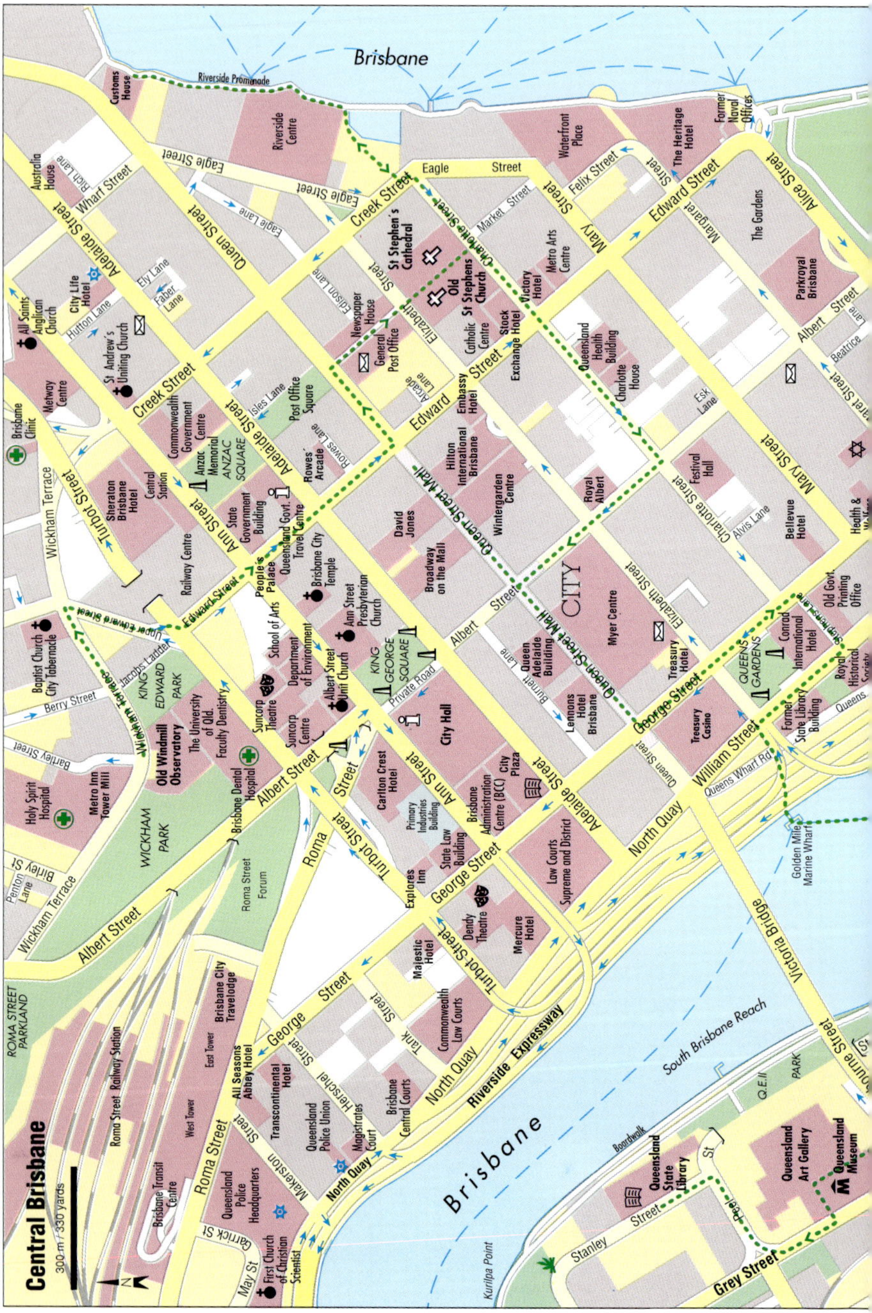
Central Brisbane
300 m / 330 yards
N
Brisbane
Riverside Promenade
Customs House
Riverside Centre
Eagle Street
Eagle Lane
Creek Street
Queen Street
Adelaide Street
Wharf Street
Rich Lane
Australia House
Ely Lane
Faber Lane
Hutton Lane
City Life Hotel
St Andrew's Uniting Church
All Saints Anglican Church
Metway Centre
Brisbane Clinic
Ann Street
Wickham Terrace
Turbot Street
Sheraton Brisbane Hotel
Central Station
Commonwealth Government Centre
Anzac Memorial
ANZAC SQUARE
Isles Lane
Post Office Square
Edison Lane
Newspaper House
General Post Office
St Stephen's Cathedral
Old St Stephens Church
Elizabeth Street
Charlotte Street
Market Street
Catholic Centre
Stock Exchange Hotel
Victory Hotel
Metro Arts Centre
Mary Street
Felix Street
Waterfront Place
The Heritage Hotel
Former Naval Offices
Edward Street
Margaret Street
The Gardens
Alice Street
Parkroyal Brisbane
Albert Street
Beatrice Lane
Arcade Lane
Embassy Hotel
Queensland Health Building
Charlotte House
Esk Lane
Howes Lane
Rowes' Arcade
State Government Building
Queensland Govt. Travel Centre
Railway Centre
Hilton International Brisbane
Wintergarden Centre
Queen Street Mall
David Jones
Broadway on the Mall
Royal Albert
Festival Hall
Alvis Lane
Bellevue Hotel
Health & Welfare
People's Palace
Brisbane City Temple
Ann Street Presbyterian Church
Edward Street
Upper Edward Street
School of Arts
Department of Environment
Albert Street Unit Church
KING GEORGE SQUARE
Private Road
City Hall
CITY
Myer Centre
Queen Adelaide Building
Burnett Lane
Treasury Hotel
QUEENS GARDENS
Conrad International Hotel
Old Govt. Printing Office
Stephens Lane
Royal Historical Society
Baptist Church City Tabernacle
Jacobs Ladder
KING EDWARD PARK
Berry Street
The University of Qld. Faculty Dentistry
Old Windmill Observatory
Suncorp Theatre
Suncorp Centre
Lennons Hotel Brisbane
George Street
Treasury Casino
Former State Library Building
Queens Wharf Rd
William Street
Barkley Street
Holy Spirit Hospital
Metro Inn Tower Mill
Brisbane Dental Hospital
Albert Street
Roma Street
Carlton Crest Hotel
Primary Industries Building
Brisbane Administration Centre (BCC)
City Plaza
North Quay
WICKHAM PARK
Birley St
Penton Lane
Roma Street Forum
State Law Building
Law Courts Supreme and District
Golden Mile Marine Wharf
Explorers Inn
Dendy Theatre
Mercure Hotel
Victoria Bridge
ROMA STREET PARKLAND
Brisbane City Travelodge
East Tower
Majestic Hotel
Commonwealth Law Courts
Tank Street
Riverside Expressway
South Brisbane Reach
All Seasons Abbey Hotel
Herschel Street
Transcontinental Hotel
West Tower
Roma Street Railway Station
Brisbane Transit Centre
Queensland Police Union
Magistrates Court
Brisbane Central Courts
Q.E.II PARK
Boardwalk
Queensland State Library
Queensland Art Gallery
Queensland Museum
Queensland Police Headquarters
Makerston Street
Garrick St
May St
First Church of Christian Scientist
Kurilpa Point
Stanley Street
Peel St
Grey Street
Melbourne Street

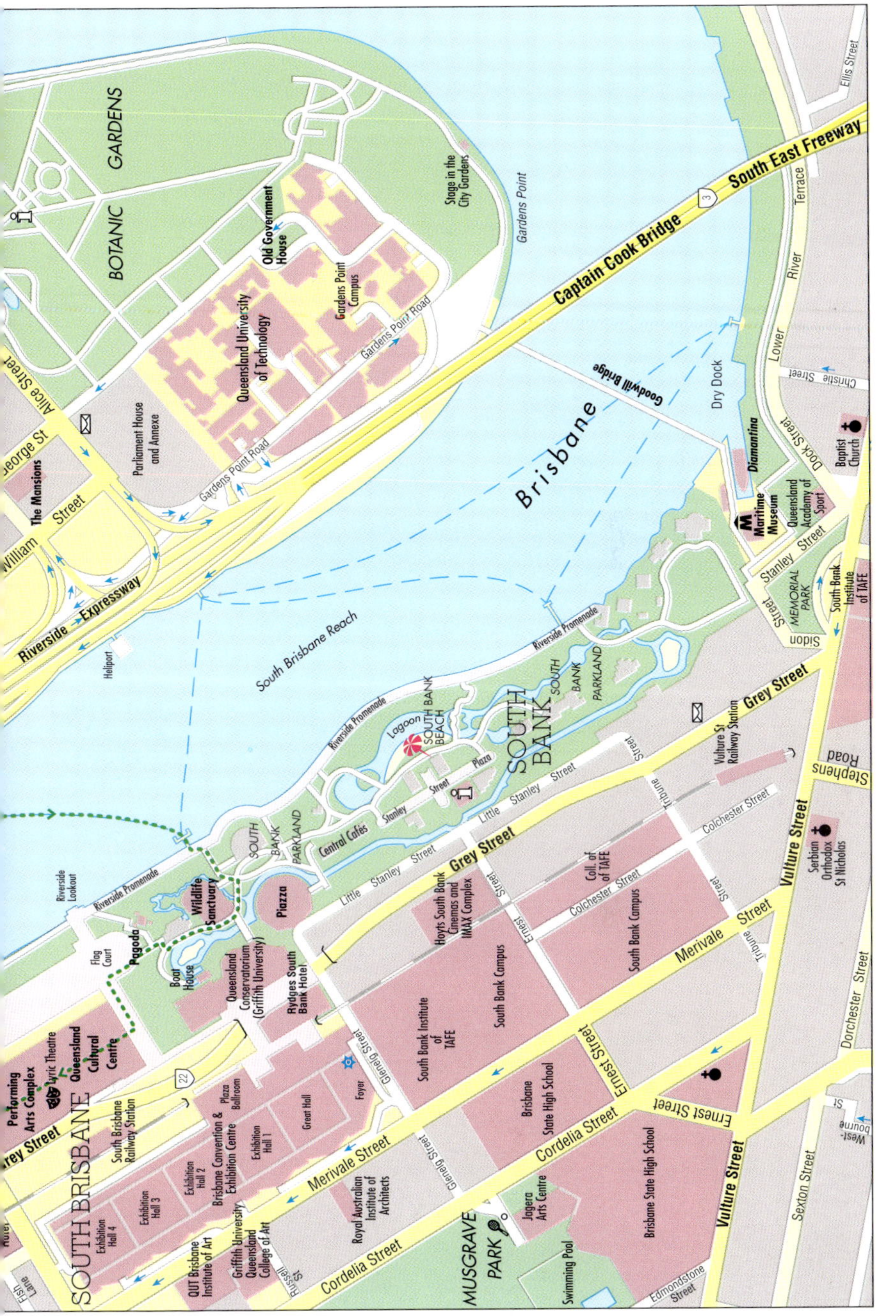
BOTANIC GARDENS
Old Government House
Queensland University of Technology
Gardens Point Campus
Gardens Point Road
Stage in the City Gardens
Gardens Point
Captain Cook Bridge
South East Freeway
Parliament House and Annexe
Alice Street
George St
The Mansions
William Street
Riverside Expressway
Heliport
South Brisbane Reach
Brisbane
Goodwill Bridge
Dry Dock
Diamantina
Maritime Museum
Queensland Academy of Sport
Lower River Terrace
Ellis Street
Christie Street
Dock Street
Baptist Church
Stanley Street
Sidon Street
MEMORIAL PARK
South Bank Institute of TAFE
Stephens Road
Riverside Promenade
SOUTH BANK PARKLAND
SOUTH BANK BEACH
Lagoon
Plaza
Stanley Street
Central Cafés
SOUTH BANK
Little Stanley Street
Grey Street
Vulture St Railway Station
Riverside Lookout
Wildlife Sanctuary
Piazza
Pagoda
Flag Court
Boat House
Queensland Conservatorium (Griffith University)
Rydges South Bank Hotel
Hoyts South Bank Cinemas and IMAX Complex
Coll. of of TAFE
Colchester Street
Tribune Street
South Bank Campus
Ernest Street
Merivale Street
Vulture Street
Serbian Orthodox St Nicholas
Dorchester Street
Performing Arts Complex
Lyric Theatre
Queensland Cultural Centre
Grey Street
SOUTH BRISBANE
South Brisbane Railway Station
Plaza Ballroom
Brisbane Convention & Exhibition Centre
Exhibition Hall 1
Exhibition Hall 2
Exhibition Hall 3
Exhibition Hall 4
Great Hall
Foyer
Glenelg Street
South Bank Institute of TAFE
Brisbane State High School
Cordelia Street
Royal Australian Institute of Architects
Griffith University Queensland College of Art
QUT Brisbane Institute of Art
Russell St
Fish Lane
MUSGRAVE PARK
Jagera Arts Centre
Swimming Pool
Brisbane State High School
Edmondstone Street
Sexton Street
West-bourne St

Brisbane

Brisbane and the Gold Coast are only about an hour's drive apart, along an excellent divided highway, mostly of eight lanes, which is virtually a freeway. This book suggests eight itineraries for visitors staying in Brisbane (including a drive up the Sunshine Coast north of the city), and six from the Gold Coast. If you're staying on the Gold Coast you can undertake any of the Brisbane itineraries after an hour's drive (or bus ride) from the Coast; vice versa if you're staying in Brisbane.

Most of Brisbane's visitor accommodation is in or close to the central business district. Many of the best locations for visitors are along or near the river, some on the opposite side of the shopping and business precinct. Given the number of itineraries described, it is well worth taking the time to familiarise yourself with the public transport system, especially the river ferries.

To Brisbane's south, the Gold Coast comprises a narrow strip of accommodation, shopping, entertainment and eating facilities – or at least that's how it might appear to the visitor. The Gold Coast actually stretches along more than 60km (37 miles) of beach from Southport to a short distance south of the New South Wales border, in most parts backed by residential development inland. Again, it's well worth getting to know the bus system.

1. Getting to Know Brisbane *(see map, p16–17)*

Spend the morning touring the city by bus; visit The Windmill, Queensland's oldest surviving building; enjoy an alfresco lunch at the Customs House brasserie or be spoilt for choice at Queen Street Mall; cross the river to admire Brisbane's stateliest buildings; visit the Wildlife Sanctuary and a clutch of museums and round off your day with an evening at the Performing Arts Complex.

Take swimming gear and wear comfortable shoes to make the most of the South Bank's 16 hectares (40 acres) of parkland

You will be travelling on an unusual-looking bus that resembles one of Brisbane's old trams (which were retired in 1969) for a **City Sights tour**. The commentary neatly blends the city's history and culture with up-to-date and informal Brisbane chat. (You may find that informality is among the most attractive aspects of this region.) Although the bus cruise allows you to set your own pace, getting on and off at any of the 19 stops on the map, it's a good idea to stay aboard and complete the round trip, which takes about 80 minutes, for an early orientation. This way you will possess enough

Left: an overview
Right: starting the day with a coffee

information on Brisbane, along with a day ticket, to launch yourself on a combined walking, bus and ferry tour of the sites that most interest you. Pick up two leaflets – a City Highlights bus leaflet and a city Heritage Trail map – at the information centre in King George Square. The first bus leaves Stop No 1, Post Office Square, at 9am; buses then run every 40 minutes until 12.20pm, and from 1.40 to 4.20pm. Your ticket is also valid on river ferries and other city buses. Visit www.brisbane.qld.gov.au for details.

Allow half a day for this leisurely exploration, which will end with lunch. If you want to follow it with another half-day itinerary (*see Contents*), your footwear should give priority to comfort ahead of style and, unusually for a city walk, you might want to pack some swimwear for a little *après*-lunch relaxation. Join the bus at Stop No 2 in Adelaide Street on **King George Square**, where **Brisbane City Hall** is the centrepiece of a diverse collection of colonial architecture. If you arrive by 8.30am (a busy time in the square as the city's commuters hurry to work), you'll have enough time to admire the building and some of its sculptures. The bronze Petrie Tableau in front of the building's façade, commissioned in Australia's bicentennial year, honours the outstanding personal achievements of the Petrie family. This distinguished clan was among Brisbane's first settlers and enjoyed an excellent relationship with the local Aborigines.

Above the building's imposing entrance, a magnificent sculpture by Daphene Mayo depicts early settlement. You might well be drawn back to this building at a later date in your stay to further appreciate its sculptures, its refurbished interior, and its **Brisbane City Gallery** (daily, 10am–8pm),

Top: seeing the city sights from a tourist bus
Left: the Windmill

which has two floors set aside for exhibitions of exclusively contemporary works in a variety of mediums. Given that Australia's recorded history and its building construction began only a little over 200 years ago, it's not surprising that the older major buildings are of various borrowed architectural styles. These combine with some superlative modern architecture in an attractive visual fusion. It's not uncommon in the busy parts of Brisbane to see aspects of the grand colonial architecture mirrored in the great expanes of glass in the city's modern towers.

Brisbane's Historic Buildings

After your round-trip tour, stay aboard the bus until you reach **The Windmill**, which is Queensland's oldest surviving building at Stop No 5, thus saving yourself a rather steep uphill walk. The mill, which was established in 1828 to grind maize into meal for the convicts, is small and unsuitable for public access, but it is a significant Brisbane landmark. It didn't work very well as a windmill due to poor design, unreliable winds, problems obtaining spare parts from faraway Sydney and a shortage of skilled millers; so the inventive jailers replaced wind power with convict power and attached a giant treadmill to the grinders. Work on the treadmill formed part of the prisoners' daily routine but, in the absence of suitable cells for solitary confinement, extended hours on the cruel device were delivered as a form of punishment for any prisoners who had the temerity to buck the system.

When the penal colony was eventually closed down, the mill was re-named the Observatory. In its new incarnation, it was used as a lookout tower from which to spot bushfires. It also became a semaphore tower with a complicated system of flags to signal the arrival and type of shipping. Its third new role was as a primitive clock. Guided by its 'time ball', a cannon would be fired every day at 1pm – a practice long since discontinued.

It's an easy downhill walk along Upper Edward Street to continue your tour. For a striking example of stately early Queensland hotel architecture, pass **Central Station** on your left, continue for another block and cross the street to the **People's Palace** on the corner of Ann Street. This edifice was built for the Salvation Army in 1911 and now provides popular low-cost backpacker accommodation. Carry on down Edward Street, and look across to **Rowes' Arcade**, an elegant pre-federation building. Turn left into Queen Street after crossing it at the lights, and halfway down the block turn right into the laneway separating another two fine old Queensland buildings – **Newspaper House** on your left and the **General Post Office** on your right.

Cross Elizabeth Street into the opposite lane, threading your way between two of Brisbane's most historic churches, **St Stephen's Cathedral** (1863) and **Old St Stephen's Church**, to reach Charlotte Street. If you

Right: St Stephen's Cathedral and Old St Stephen's Church

want to dine in **The Customs House** brasserie, take a detour by turning left in Charlotte Street, crossing Creek Street, walking through the open spaces (which may be occupied by the come-and-go markets) and along the river-bank to the left to reach the stately, copper-domed building. Art lovers will appreciate the gallery, which mostly exhibits Queensland artists, and it's also a delightful alfresco lunch option (*see Eating Out, page 74*). Here you can contemplate a small but fascinating display of historic maritime-museum artefacts including the likes of a British code-of-conduct booklet entitled *Treatment of Neutral and Enemy Merchant Ships in Time of War*.

If you'd prefer a more public luncheon venue with a greater variety of attractions, head for Queen Street Mall: backtrack up Charlotte Street, staying on the right side so that, half a block after crossing Edward Street, you'll have a fine view of two more of Brisbane's elegant buildings – the **State Health Building** (part of whose façade has been retained, with a new high-rise built behind it) and the adjacent **Charlotte House**, built in1886. Turn right at Albert Street, which will take you right into the centre of the **Queen Street Mall**. This pedestrian mall, which runs between George and Edward streets, is a communal focal point, and an optimum spot for shopping and lunching. It occupies the street frontage in which a fire destroyed almost the entire city block contained by George, Queen, Albert and Elizabeth streets in 1864. This was the country's worst fire up to that time. By the time you read this, the whole mall will have undergone a complete refurbishment. This fine mall was relatively new even before the refurbishment, and all of its best facilities were due to be reinstated in time for the re-opening.

Choose a Lunch

For lunch, try any of the high-quality outlets that also cater for Brisbane's city workers. There is little point in phoning ahead to book – it's not that kind of scene. Customers walk in off the street with the easy informality that typifies the city. The quantity and variety of food might give you the impression that Brisbane's population does nothing but eat. The competition is intense, the service can be anything from self-serve and buffet to *à la carte*, and the options are endless. The **Myer Centre Eatery** is an excellent place to start. It has an enormous food court on Level E, the street level off Queen Street, and offers virtually every type of food imaginable: Asian, Mexican, gourmet sandwiches, health foods, kebabs and so on.

A Chinese outlet called **The Orient Express** is one of a dozen or more that are unlikely to disappoint you. A little further up-market, **Jo Jo's** in the **Pavilion Building** heads the locals' popularity list. This restaurant overlooks the entire mall, enabling you to observe the thronging mass from the comfort of an elevated vantage point. Jo Jo's has a selection of Asian and other ethnic styles, as well as modern Australian, and is fully licensed. **Jimmy's on the Mall**, also licensed, is a fashionable choice right in the heart of the

Above: a seafood platter and a glass of local wine

mall; it is fully *à la carte* and its specialities include a wide range of Queensland seafoods. **Eatz on Broadway**, at **Broadway on the Mall**, is another local favourite, with an extensive ice-creamery, a couple of excellent coffee shops and Japanese gourmet restaurants. Look out for special offers such as The Eatery's 'two-dollar Tuesday', when all meals are sold for $2.

Across the River

Before you cross the river, take a little time to admire a cluster of Brisbane's stateliest buildings, which were not included earlier in the day's itinerary. The Italianate **Treasury Casino**, originally the State Treasury, was erected in three stages from 1885 to 1928 on the site of the former convict-built guard houses, officers' quarters and military barracks. The accommodation was set behind arches and colonnades that protected it from the sun and rain but did not obstruct cooling ventilation. Also take in the three former government institutions built in complementary styles – the **State Library Building**,which now houses assorted government departments; the **Land Administration Building**, now a hotel associated with the casino; and **Government Printing Office**, now home to the Sciencentre.

You can take a ferry across the river from North Quay at the end of Elizabeth Street to our next dallying-point – the 16-hectare (40-acre) **South Bank Parkland**. (To reach the ferry wharf, continue along William Street to Queen Street, make a left U-turn into Queens Wharf Road, and take the steps on your right.) If the 25–30 minute interval between ferries doesn't fit your schedule, a 10-minute scenic walk across the Victoria Bridge or the new Goodwill walking bridge from the Botanical Gardens to the Maritime Museum at South Bank will provide some splendid city views.

South Bank is Brisbane's former World Expo site, now wholly revamped with parks, tropical gardens, lagoons and yet more dining precincts. You could easily spend a whole day or more there without

Above: South Bank Parkland
Right: a golden bird on a golden coast

finding yourself in the same place twice. Settle for spending the afternoon there, choosing from the available attractions and refreshment options on site. You might want to return for a night at the theatre. A 24-hour entertainment infoline (tel: 3867 2020) gives you a somewhat vague outline of day-to-day activities, whereas the Visitor Information Centre (tel: 3867 2051) goes into more detail on what options and attractions are available on a particular day. These include swimming or sunbathing by a sandy, safe pool right across the river from the city, with a beach patrolled by a lifeguard (although the water is shallow and safe) during the summer. Other South Bank features include a **Wildlife Sanctuary** (9am–5pm), which is home to a number of Australian birds and animals, and the **IMAX theatre** (open daily with shows every hour).

Cultural Attractions

South Bank is the venue of both the **Queensland Cultural Centre** and the **Queensland Art Gallery** (daily, 10am–5pm; tel: 3840 7303; free except for special exhibitions), which is one of the most prestigious art galleries in the entire country. In addition to its extensive permanent collections of Australian, Aboriginal, European and Asian works, the gallery has a reputation for securing exhibitions of major Australian artists (including Lloyd Rees and Arthur Streeton) and for putting on outstanding international exhibitions.

The adjacent **Queensland Museum** (daily 9.30am–5pm; tel: 3840 7555; free except for special exhibitions) brings together a fascinating collection of natural history exhibits, focusing on both the folk history of the country's indigenous people and the very different experience of the early European settlers. From the call of the humpback whales suspended near the museum's entrance to pioneering Queensland

Top: outdoor entertainment, South Bank
Left: Chinese exhibits in Queensland Museum

aviator Bert Hinkler's fragile biplane, the Queensland Museum offers education and entertainment against an Australian backdrop.

The **Maritime Museum** (9.30am–5pm; excluding Good Friday and Anzac Day morning; tel: 3844 5361) focuses on Queensland's close links with the seaways and its dependence on them, then and now. Ever since the Dutch explorer Willem Janssen and the crew of the *Duyfken* landed on Cape York Peninsula in 1606, the sea has shaped Queenslanders' lives and commerce. The museum features a wealth of artefacts reflecting the state's maritime history. These include the World War II frigate *Diamantina*, the 1924 steam tug *Forceful*, and a late 19th-century pearling lugger.

The magnificent **Queensland Performing Arts Complex** hosts a wide range of world-class theatrical productions in four theatres. The complex also includes two restaurants, a coffee shop and a gift shop. Check the info-line (*see page 24*) for events during your visit to the city. The nearby **Queensland State Library** (weekdays 9am–5pm), at the western end of the Cultural Centre, offers not only panoramic city views, but is also a treasure trove of books, journals, newspapers and CDs. It also offers access to the National Film Archive, Internet links to international databases and a wealth of historical items at the John Oxley Library, Queensland's most authoritative source of historical information.

Much of Brisbane's local art is influenced by the evolution of a bright, distinctive Queensland style, moulded by the mountains, sea, rainforests and deserts that together form Queensland's diverse environment. There is also a strong strand of more conceptually-based work and a fine representation of Aboriginal art. The established inner suburbs, in particular New Farm, Newstead and Fortitude Valley, are home to a flourishing community of artists whose media include sculpture, paintings and crafts.

Saleable Art

The hub of Brisbane's saleable art is Brunswick Street in Fortitude Valley and neighbouring New Farm, which is close to the city and, in an area dotted with restaurants, cafés and bistros, easily accessible by public transport (including the fast, quiet Rivercat ferries). These locations are loosely described as the **Art Gallery Circuit**. As if averse to permanence, galleries tend to come and go, so it's impossible to produce a comprehensive guide, but about 17 galleries co-operate to help the visitor identify all the studios on the circuit. These consist of government funded/supported exhibition rooms (some of which sell work) and private commercial galleries.

The Institute of Modern Art, 608 Ann Street, Fortitude Valley (Tues–Fri 11am–5pm, Sat 11am–4pm; tel: 3252 5750) is a non-commercial public gallery with a focus on experimental art. Also worth a visit is the **Crafts**

Right: gallery crafts in Brunswick Market

Queensland Gallery (381 Brunswick Street; tel: 1800 172080) which hosts exhibitions of work for sale, as well as continuously displaying a wide range of art products at an equally wide range of prices. Within the Brunswick Street precinct alone – accessible on foot or by taxi – you can run the gamut of contemporary art, from expensive works by well-established Australian artists, such as Margaret Olley and Jeffrey Smart, to more affordable works by contemporary artists, and high-quality local craft work.

The Phillip Bacon Gallery exhibits good contemporary Australian and overseas art for the serious collector, while Joe Airo-Farulla's **Gallery 482** (at 482 Brunswick Street) is one of the most established on the circuit, specialising in contemporary art predominantly from Australia and in all media, but also from New Zealand and occasionally New Caledonia, the UK and elsewhere. Airo-Farulla tends to focus on more challenging work and the art he displays is a reliable guide to what collectors are buying.

2. Saving the Whales *(see map, p27)*

A day trip by catamaran to Moreton Island; explore Cape Moreton on foot; go whale-watching at Tangalooma; hand-feed the dolphins; laze in the altogether on the beach at Lucinda Bay; snorkel among The Wrecks or try your hand at sand-tobogganing.

Depart from Tangalooma launch terminal at Pinkenba on the lower Brisbane River or take the courtesy bus from the Brisbane Transit Centre in Roma Street. Day tours by catamaran take about 75 minutes.

As recently as 40 years ago, visitors to Brisbane used to cross Moreton Bay to Tangalooma on **Moreton Island** to witness the gruesome spectacle of slaughtered whales being butchered for processing into products such as edible oils, whaleboned garments and high-protein livestock food. The settlement that is now the **Tangalooma Wild Dolphin Resort** (tel: 3268 6333; www.tangalooma.com) occupies the former site of one of the world's largest whaling stations, established there in 1952, because it lay conveniently

close to the narrow deep-water channel along which about 10,000 humpback whales migrated every year. Ten years after the whaling station was established, it was estimated that just 500 humpbacks remained. Soon after, the authorities put a stop to all whaling from Tangalooma.

Shell middens (huge mounds of seashells marking the former dining quarters of Aboriginal tribes) and other archaeological evidence show that Aborigines occupied Moreton Island for at least 1,500 years. It was the ready supply of fish, shellfish and other foods on and around the island that attracted the Ngugi people. Later, as was the practice along the Queensland coast, goats and pigs were released on the island to breed, thereby providing emergency rations for sailors unlucky enough to be shipwrecked there. Although the idea had good intentions, it turned out to be an act of environmental vandalism. This created an ongoing problem because the feral pigs and cats that are common throughout Queensland make life difficult for native wildlife as well as for vegetation and conservation.

Moreton Island played a military role in both world wars; and it was during the latter conflict that some infrastructure foundations for the ill-fated whaling station were laid. Sand-mining exploration began on the island in 1947, but despite the mineral-richness of the dunes, only small areas were ever mined, and conservationists succeeded in having the area closed to mining when it reverted to its function as a national park. Today the island is 97 percent national park, almost all of which is a huge and mostly forested sand mass.

The exception is **Cape Moreton**, at the island's northern extremity, the rocky barrier against which the sea-washed white sand has, over the years, piled up to form an island with no less than 185km (115 miles) of sandy beaches. A variety of several walking tracks offers a choice of bush, beach and bay views from specially constructed lookouts – get a walking map from the resort

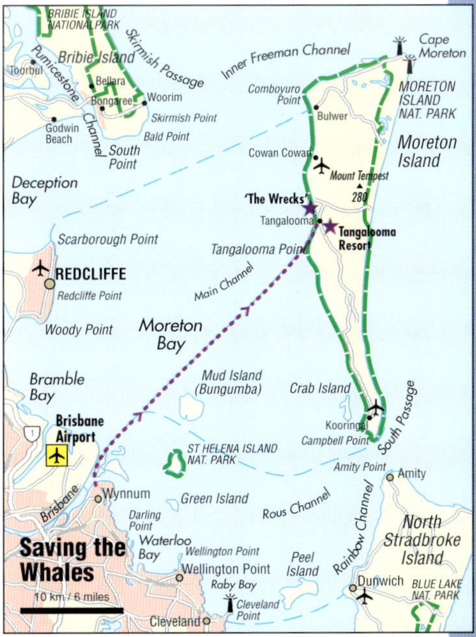

Left: sand tobogganing
Above: bottlenose dolphins

before you set out. Whales (a category that includes the bottlenose dolphin, which is one of the 70-odd whale species) are still among Tangalooma's main attractions, but now we visit them only on the friendliest of terms and target them with telescopic lenses rather than explosive harpoons.

These giant aquatic mammals, some weighing more than 50 tonnes, choose sheltered havens such as Tangalooma in which to rest during their long migratory journeys. Small groups ('pods') of whales begin their migration in the Antarctic, where they spend the summer feeding, and travel to the warmer winter waters of the Great Barrier Reef where the eligible individuals court, noisily but unintelligibly, before mating; maybe they are emulating the behaviour patterns of some of the region's human visitors. The young whales are the first to leave the Antarctic, followed by the mature cows and bulls. Bringing up the rear come the pregnant females, which will give birth in the north before returning with their young to their summer feeding grounds. A pod normally comprises just two or three whales, but sometimes several pods can be seen travelling together. According to recent estimates, the annually migrating humpback population has recovered to the extent that there are now around 3,000 of these magnificent creatures. Observing humpbacks happily swimming in their natural environment has proved far more popular among tourists than witnessing their reduction to saleable commodities.

A day at Tangalooma can be as leisurely or as action-packed as you choose. (There is also the option of staying overnight to hand-feed the wild dolphins and to relax in an understated and genuinely friendly resort.) The attractions vary from day to day, however, so take care to identify a day that matches your preference.

Top: Cape Moreton Island Lighthouse
Left: ready to take the plunge

All cruises depart from the Tangalooma launch terminal at Pinkenba, on the lower Brisbane River. Be sure to book in advance. A courtesy bus will pick up passengers from several city hotels and from the Brisbane Transit Centre in Roma Street, and the reservations operator will let you know your nearest pick-up point. Day tours operate seven days a week via a high-speed catamaran which makes the trip in about 75 minutes. You'll almost certainly need sun-screen, but if you forget to take it, you can buy it on the island. Fins, masks and snorkels can be hired at the watersports outlet, as can catamarans, windsurfers, dinghies and fishing equipment. Introductory SCUBA, sailing, snorkelling and water-ski lessons are also available (book ahead on the resort number). Take comfortable walking shoes, and, of course, swimwear, unless you are bold enough to walk an extra 15 minutes or so south to one of the secluded beaches of **Lucinda Bay**, beyond Shark Spit, where swimwear is optional. A range of reasonably priced eating options, from snacks and sandwiches to full meals, is available.

Although protected from the open sea, the Moreton Bay crossing can occasionally be choppy. But, guided by a skilled skipper sensitive to the passengers' comfort, the catamaran smoothes out most of the lurches. The route passes St Helena Island, the site of a very prisoner-unfriendly colonial correction centre which continued to operate for years after England ceased populating Australia with its less privileged citizens.

Watch a Whale

Whale-watching is available daily in season from mid-June to the end of October. A tour is the most popular option. If you have a booking, stay aboard the catamaran, on which a light lunch is served. The whale-spotting success rate is extremely high, not least because whale-watchers share their information. The Tangalooma spotter plane also increases the probability of a sighting. In the last year for which statistics are available, whales were spotted on all but two of 52 trips. Other whale species, including the very rare great southern white whale, are occasionally seen, not only on the ocean side, but in the bay itself, where some have been known to spend a day or two resting close to the resort. Also growing in numbers are orca 'killer whales', the humpbacks' natural enemies, whose presence indicates that the balance of nature is now overcoming the adverse effects of human intervention. There is a whole whale-watcher's vocabulary to describe the creatures' various acrobatic manoeuvres as they broach the surface: doubtless your expert commentators will enlighten you.

Swimming at the resort itself is safe because there is very little tidal flow. The 37-km (23-mile) ocean side (which you won't see on a normal day's visit) is remote and unattended by lifeguards, has strong tides and 'rips', and is definitely unsafe. One kilometre (½ mile) north of the resort is an

Right: coming up for air

artificial reef of deliberately sunken ships, including at least two retired whalers, where submerged old vessels form an anchorage for visiting craft. **The Wrecks** also add interest to snorkelling. This snorkelling is best done as a guided activity and can be pre-arranged through the resort.

Sand-tobogganing

If you're not at Tangalooma in the whale-watching season, you should, if you're feeling adventurous, try your hand at sand-tobogganing. A huge but cleverly-driven four-wheel-drive bus bounces you halfway across the island, through a fascinating range of Aussie bush environments, to 'the desert', which is in fact a 42-hectare (100-acre) sand blow. This is a series of huge barren dunes of slowly-drifting beach sand surrounded by the forested sand-hills that make up the island. As the bus emerges from the shadowy bush, your eyes will be dazzled by the sudden whiteness of the dunes. Your guide will probably dig a few shallow holes in the ground with his hands, extracting different coloured handfuls of mineral sand, explaining the sand's origins and demonstrating some of its unusual qualities.

All that sand-tobogganing requires is a waxed sheet of particle-board (supplied), an eager participant, some cursory instructions, and a gentle shove – and you are on an exhilarating slide down the leeward side of a dune, reaching speeds of about 60kph (40mph) with nothing to fear but a mouthful of sand if you don't correctly follow instructions.

Whether you have been sand-tobogganing or whale-watching, you return to Tangalooma with an hour to spare before the catamaran leaves on its return trip. There's usually a **Heliquest** helicopter based there (tel: 3880 2229) and if you have the time and the cash, a quick aerial flit across this amazing island is a worthwhile addition to your day's experience.

You will be back at the Brisbane terminal at 4.45pm, except on Saturday when the return boat leaves and arrives one hour later. The extra hour makes Saturday the most popular day for the visitor who has a choice.

3. Sunshine Coast Day Tour (see map, p32)

Steal a glimpse of the Glass House Mountains; penetrate 'the bush'; visit Mary Cairncross Park and the two hill towns of Maleny and Montville; have a fruity lunch in the Big Pineapple; visit the Ginger Factory; head for the spectacular surf beaches; swim and relax.

This day trip along the coast north of Brisbane offers an insight into the relatively low impact that civilisation has had on this vast land, as well as putting the accomplishments of its explorers into perspective.

There are no coach tours along this route, so you will need to hire a car, and you'll be driving about 300km (186 miles) but with plenty of breaks. Your drive north from Brisbane is best begun early: try to be on the road by 8am to allow yourself a leisurely day, but if you do sleep in, a 9am departure will still allow reasonable time to take in the day's attractions. Remember to check the weather forecast the previous day because the mist that sometimes shrouds the hills along this route spoils the views. And the beaches are best enjoyed in the golden sunshine after which the coast was named.

If the weather is fine, and if you can afford to spoil yourself at a slight premium, hire a lovingly maintained topless vintage or current touring car – anything from a two-seater Ford Capri to a Cadillac Eldorado which is uncrowded with six aboard – from **Roadsters** (Mon–Fri 8am–5pm, Sat and Sun 8am–4pm; tel: 3252 3833). There are innumerable and varied eating options along the route at moderate prices. If you would rather be independent, you could ask your hotel to pack you some light refreshments and cold drinks in an icebox, or an 'esky' as Australians would have it.

Pick up Lutwyche Road, which takes you out of the inner suburbs and becomes Gympie Road. It's marked as Route 3, but becomes Highway One at the Redcliffe exit. Most of the morning traffic is inbound to the city, so northbound lanes are relatively uncrowded. The route is well signposted, but remember to take a map. You should avoid the temptation to exceed the speed limits, even though they are rarely higher than 100kph (60mph), because there are speed cameras along this route. If you get a fine, the hire-car company will pay it and bill your credit card.

The Stuff of Legend

About 54km (33 miles) north of Brisbane, turn off the Bruce Highway at the well-marked Landsborough exit and take the **Glass House Mountains** Road to Landsborough. You'll catch your first good glimpses of the Glass House Mountains – steep-sided volcanic cores so named because of tricks

Left: Tangalooma beach
Top: firm friends. **Right**: a classic hire car

of reflected light on the rain-damped peaks, first noted by Captain Cook from offshore, and the stuff of Aboriginal legend. You're now well into the bush, and will see, interspersed with pine plantations, extensive tracts of typical native vegetation. These will give you a perception of the challenges faced by the region's early explorers and settlers as they hacked their way through that trackless wilderness, leading packhorses, without a map or a known destination. The Glass House Mountains' well-drained slopes of rich volcanic soil are ideal for growing pineapples, which are sold at numerous roadside stalls, along with avocados and other locally grown fruit. The region is also the native home of the Queensland nut, now better known worldwide as the macadamia nut.

For the best views of the region's geological showpiece, continue past the township of Glass House Mountains to Landsborough, ignoring signs advertising other vantage points. From here the road begins a slow climb through virgin bush, winding up the ridge towards Maleny (rhymes with 'zany'). As you climb higher, there are more and more views of the placid farming valleys below, and the coastline to the east. The ascending road is well-maintained, and safe as long as you are careful. Drivers don't have to miss out on the views – there are plenty of spots to stop and take photographs, or just to admire the countryside.

Watch for Cairncross Corner, and turn left there from the main Maleny road, following the signs to **Mary Cairncross Park**, about 2km (just over a mile) along that road. You should reach the

Right: Glass House Mountains

park, which has a kiosk and facilities, within 90 minutes of leaving Brisbane. From the park, there's an unobstructed view of the farming valleys in the foreground, the Glass House Mountains in the middle distance, the coastline to the left and maybe, on a clear day, Brisbane to the south. Continue on the same road, following the marked tourist drive, to the hill township of **Maleny**. A picturesque country town, its early colonial architecture has been well preserved. It's the kind of place to which you might like to retire to do all the things you never had time for – its population includes any number of artists and craftsmen who've done just that. Local craft products sold in the shops range from rustic log furniture to fireside bellows crafted from red cedar and she-oak. You might want to take advantage of the opportunity to buy something genuinely Australian at a reasonable price.

Four kilometres (2½ miles) along another ridge road is the left turn to Montville, which is 11km (7 miles) further on. Again you'll enjoy spectacular ridge-top vistas of the coast and hinterland, and a few glimpses of the scenic Lake Baroon reservoir. **Montville**, which is even prettier than Maleny, puts on a slightly more polished performance for the visitor. Its main street is ornamented with determinedly quaint shopfronts, offering a wealth of variety in local craftwork, and a range of tempting kerbside eateries.

A Fruitful Encounter

Your browsing in Maleny and Montville is likely to keep you busy until lunch time, and you still have the tranquil splendours of the Sunshine Coast's under-crowded beaches to look forward to. Take the Woombye–Montville Road, and wend your way down the pleasant but rather steep descent (drive in a low gear) and stop after 17km (10 miles). This is a good time to take a breather. A huge and quite realistic-looking fibreglass pineapple, constructed as a roadside ornament, heralds **The Big Pineapple** (9am–5pm; daily buffet 11.30am–2.30pm; tel: 5442 1333). Should you enter this mammoth fruit, educational videos will assail you with all sorts of information about the pineapple-growing industry. The spacious, airy dining room overlooks the plantation and the green jungle perimeter.

The dining room features a plethora of perfect parfaits and seductive sundaes, with a strong emphasis on the region's tropical fruits, including bananas, ginger, macadamias, mangoes, and pineapples. In addition to the buffet, there's a licensed restaurant downstairs near the railway station.

Take the new freeway section of the Bruce Highway northwards to Yandina, where you leave the freeway to drive through a rural landscape to **Coolum Beach**. A 'brown sign' at the highway exit may tempt you to pay a quick visit to **The Ginger Factory** at Yandina to stock up on locally-produced chocolate-coated ginger. If you are not tempted to deviate, the whole drive should take you less than 40 minutes. You are then rewarded by vistas of almost endless and underpopulated surf beaches, broken only by a handful of small headlands which offer breathtaking beach views.

Safe Swimming

The rest of the afternoon is yours to cruise this beautiful coastline, from Noosa, about 15km (9 miles) north, to **Caloundra**, which is 30km (18 miles) south. You might want to embark on a pleasant stroll on any of the coast's beautiful beaches; alternatively, you could take the opportunity to go for a swim. If you decide on the latter option, remember that the only safe swimming locations are those patrolled by surf lifesavers. This is a year-round service, provided by volunteer lifesavers during the summer and local government patrols at other times. When a beach is patrolled, it's only safe to swim in the water between the flags. From north to south, the patrolled beaches are Noosa Heads, Sunshine Beach, Peregian Beach, Coolum Beach, Marcoola, Mudjimba, Maroochydore, Alexandra Headland, Mooloolaba, Kawana Waters, North Caloundra and Metropolitan Caloundra. The friendly surf lifesaving clubs welcome anyone in need of refreshments and bar service.

If you've left yourself enough time, follow the coast road all the way to Caloundra, stopping wherever the coastal scenery appeals. If you're running late, the Sunshine Coast Motorway, which runs parallel to the coast, leads you more speedily to the highway for your return to Brisbane. The drive from Caloundra to Brisbane city should take less than an hour and a half.

Top: beach life, Caloundra
Left: the Big Pineapple train

4. Stately Timber Architecture (see map, p36)

Walk through the localities of Brisbane's earliest settlements; pay a visit to Government House where the flag flies only when the governor is in residence; admire the old 'tin and timber' Queenslander buildings; sample the local brew in the many popular watering-holes.

The value Queenslanders place on their early building styles is reflected in the retention of original facades.

Several of Brisbane's inner suburbs, among them Hamilton, Newstead and New Farm, are similar to the one you're about to explore. In the later months of the year, especially September to November, your visit will be enhanced by the rich mauve blooms of native jacaranda trees and some imported species, including the scarlet poinciana and the bright yellow cassia.

On this short (50–60-minute) walk through some of Brisbane's earliest-settled localities, you will sample Queensland's distinctive architectural styles from around the beginning of the 20th century. While there was still vacant land there, most early residents built their settlements as 'ribbon developments' along the breezy ridge lines of the hilly terrain that much of Brisbane occupies. You'll be walking along one of these routes back to the city centre, so, rather than taking a taxi ride along the same route, ask the driver to go via Milton Road, where you will also see the imposing building which houses Castlemaine Perkins' XXXX (Four-ex) brewery. (Southerners like to joke that the state's most popular beverage is called XXXX because its devotees can't spell beer.)

Colonial Tradition

Ask the cab to turn into Baroona Road, which later becomes Fernberg Road, and to deposit you at the gatekeeper's lodge at **Government House**. Built originally for a prominent parliamentarian around 1865 and named Fernberg, this is one of Brisbane's most elegant residences, and the home of the state governor – the Queen's representative in the state of Queensland. Uniquely, because a former conservative government saw republicanism coming and enacted legislation, Queensland will remain a dominion of England, and the governor will retain his status, in the event of a republic being declared. So the Queensland flag flies from the tower and, in a fine display of colonial tradition, the governor's flag flies only while he is in residence.

The other unusual aspect of this residence is that it is not made of timber. In early Brisbane timber was cheap, carpenters were plentiful or easy to train, and the skills and raw materials required for brick and stone buildings were so much rarer that only a handful of the first major buildings were of masonry; the rest were 'timber and tin'.

Continue up the hill to the west for several other views of Government House and its manicured grounds and lawns where formal garden parties are

Right: Government House

held. The garden includes an elegant row of black ironbark (*Eucalyptus Decepta*) – one of about 700 eucalyptus species native to Australia. Turn right and walk just one block up the only slightly steep hill of this walk, to a roundabout, where you turn right again into Latrobe Terrace. (Brisbane has a somewhat confusing habit of changing the name of a contiguous thoroughfare every few blocks, and this one will become Given Terrace, then Caxton Street, during your short walk.)

Perched on the highest points of the ridge line and clinging to the lower slopes on either side, is a wide range of federation-style 'timber and tin' architecture. Extraordinarily long stumps – up to perhaps 15 metres (45ft) – are used to support the downhill sides of some of these residences and to provide a level floor platform for the structure of the house, expressing an Australian preference for single-floor homes. 'Houses on stilts' are common throughout early and even contemporary Queensland architecture, but there are discernible shifts in architectural fashion over the period during which timber construction dominated.

In one of the earlier styles, the weatherboard is attached to the *inside* of the exposed timber frame, and is of weatherboard shape externally, while its other side provides a smooth inner wall. This design saved timber, provided a quick means of cooling at night, and also avoided the kind of dark

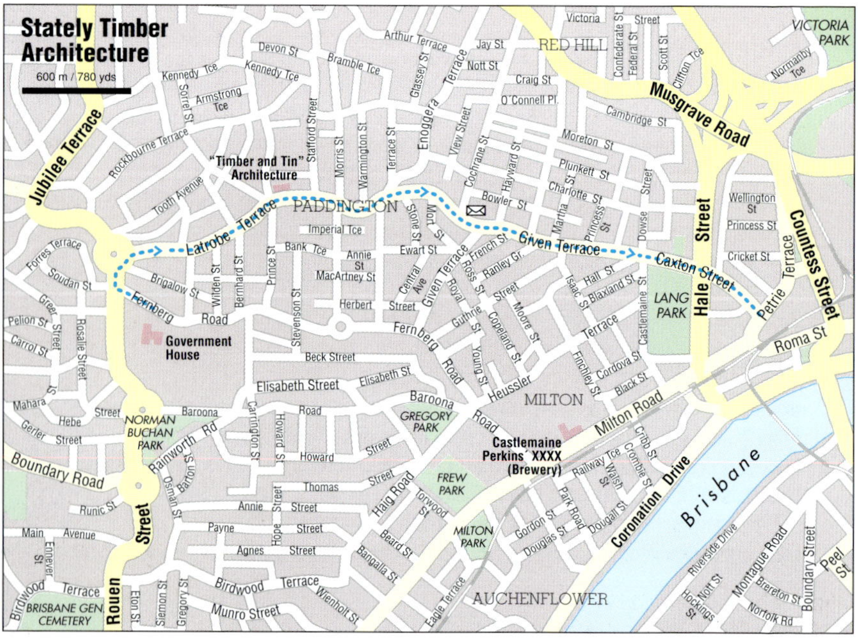

and unventilated spaces in which permanent damp and mildew could rot the structure – a common threat given the state's tropical and subtropical climates. On many houses, the external ornament is exclusively timber, with combinations of shaped lattice and fretwork panels, and lathed supports, producing a 'wood lace' visual effect. In the more elaborate structures, cast-iron fretwork is used to add to this effect, and mass-produced casement windows decorated with coloured panels are common, as are pressed-metal ceilings, which you will see in several shops that were converted from residences. The value Queenslanders place on their early building styles is reflected in the retention of original façades and in the use of colonial-style themes in new homes. Much of the timber is from tree species such as Queensland red cedar and silky oak, both of which are now protected.

Restoration Activity

The traffic is not a serious problem, but do take care crossing and recrossing the road, as you will want to do. Although the buildings along this walk speak for themselves, take a look at No 198 Latrobe Terrace for a fine example of the caring restoration of an old Queenslander, as early residences are collectively described, especially by estate agents. In the nearby but less opulent areas of the city, there are many neglected-looking tin and timber homes evidently in need of – or undergoing – this type of restoration. Australian artists have become adept at portraying the various iron-oxide hues which characterise their elderly corrugated iron roofs.

Antiques shops, featuring interior rather than exterior restoration, are a feature of the walk, and well worth a browse for their displays of furniture and ornament, which match the architecture for diversity. Half a dozen such shops are clustered around the intersection of Latrobe Terrace with Prince Street. The route also takes in a wealth of specialised antiques shops (or in some cases, 'shoppes') that stock out-of-print books, musical instruments, gramophone records and other treasures from the past. There's even an Olde Refrigerator Shoppe. Just beyond the Paddington Market, look to the left down Great George Street for a hillside vista of old Queenslanders.

On this walk you won't need to carry refreshments; there is a vast range of restaurants, alfresco coffee shops and eateries. A popular pub, the **Paddo** (a typical abbreviation for Paddington) is conveniently situated mid-route. There is also a wide range of New Age establishments offering such alternative diversions as acupuncture, aromatherapy, astrology, meditation, crystal-gazing, palmistry, and pyramid-power.

The huge stadium to your right is **Lang Park**, the home of Queensland rugby league. It's also called The Cauldron and is the venue of Queensland football's major confrontations. On your left is a small park, featuring huge Moreton Bay figs and other ficus species, which are a feature of Queensland's rainforests. This is a sign that you're approaching Caxton Street. Here you will find a number of pubs and outdoor restaurants, of which the first on the right, The Caxton, is highly recommended.

Above left: old Queenslanders, Paddington
Right: a toast to a famous Australian lager

5. Views, Gardens and the Riverside *(see map, p39)*

Inspect the city from the heights of Mount Coot-tha; move on to the Botanical Gardens via the J.C. Slaughter Falls and take in the starry entertainment of the Sir Thomas Brisbane Planetarium. From the Regatta Hotel, continue along the river to the South Bank Parkland.

Good walking shoes are a must for this pedestrian option, which begins in the bush at Brisbane's back door. An after-breakfast start will extend your range of options, allowing you to make it a whole day if you so wish. However, an afternoon walk is equally enjoyable unless it's very hot. At the weekend there is plenty of river activity to see on the way.

This walk is from Mount Coot-tha to the Botanical Gardens, then along the Brisbane River to the **South Bank Parkland** where you can relax before deciding whether to call it a day. It's important to understand that there is another park often called 'the botanical gardens' that adjoins the city centre in the river loop. Although that park is certainly a pleasant place, it is not the real Botanical Gardens, which you will visit during this walk.

Take a taxi to the top of **Mount Coot-tha**, from where you can gain an overview of the city and its surroundings from a special viewing area. Refreshments are available from several outlets. Opened in 1976, the location attracts more than half a million people annually. The footpath down the hill (it's not *really* a mountain) to the **J.C. Slaughter Falls** is an easy walk that takes about half an hour through natural Australian bushland. Unfortunately you might not be rewarded by the sight of an active waterfall because the flow is seasonal.

From the Falls it's only another 800 metres (2,620ft) to Brisbane's 52-hectare (128-acre) **Botanical Gardens** (8am–5.30pm, but closing 5pm from April to August). These gardens, in which the plants are separated into native and exotic collections, are truly world-class in terms of variety and presentation. They feature such diverse microclimates as tropical rainforest, desert tropical, tropical wet, tropical dry, lagoon and marsh, attracting a wide variety of birds. Be sure to pick up a self-guiding map at the information

Above: an overview from Mount Coot-tha
Right: J. C. Slaughter Falls bushwalk

centre, because the gardens are vast and you may well become hopelessly lost. Follow the White Arrow Trail marked in the leaflet, which will guide you along a representative path, taking about an hour if you resist the temptation to explore some of the gardens' alluring byways.

Be sure to visit the **Fragrant Plant & Herb Garden**, where the aromas of dozens of culinary, fragrant and medicinal herbs, as well as flowers, will delight your senses. You will be invited to smell the blossoms in season, and gently rub the leaves of the assorted mints, lavenders and other plants. The gardens have cleverly exploited Brisbane's climate to allow the growth, in separate sections, of: tropical vegetation (in a humidified dome); arid-region cacti and succulents; a Japanese garden that was given to the city by the Japanese government; and an exotic rainforest containing an assorted collection of species from around the world. Botanical enthusiasts should check (tel: 3403 2535; www.brisbane.qld.gov.au) whether the gardens are running any special botanical exhibition activities.

While you are visiting the gardens, the **Sir Thomas Brisbane Planetarium** gives you the chance to explore the heavens in its Cosmic Skydome. Here you can experience the dark tranquillity of space, even on the sunniest day. The space observation lasts about 45 minutes, changes throughout the year, and is not recommended for children under the age of six. Of special interest to visitors from the northern hemi-

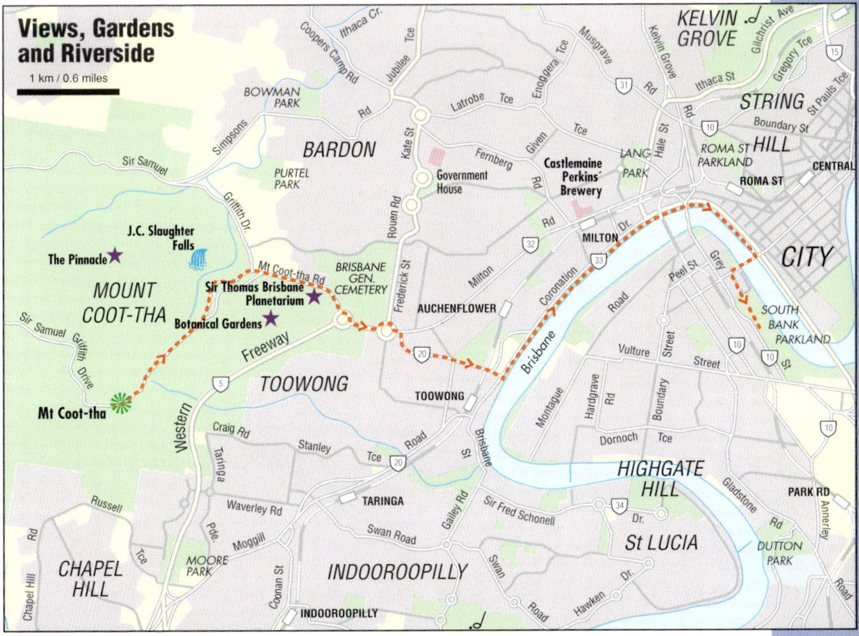

sphere unfamiliar with the south's stellar patterns is a re-creation of each night's Brisbane sky projected on the dome. General programmes are at 3.30pm Wed–Fri; 1.30, 3.30 and 7.30pm Sat;1.30 and 3pm Sun; closed Mon and Tues. (For updated timing of shows, which vary during school holidays, and for bookings, tel: 3403 2578.)

The **Planetarium Lakeside Restaurant** is open daily 9.30am–4.30pm, except Sun, when it opens at 8.30am and there's a barbecue buffet breakfast and lunch.

Beginning your onward walk, there is a good footpath on the left of Mount Coot-tha Road, but if you walk on the unpaved right-hand side you'll be rewarded by some lovely outside-looking-in views of the Botanical Gardens. At the intersection of Frederick Street, there's an overpass and a roundabout. Stay at street level and be careful of traffic coming off the roundabout. A block further on, cross the road and take the half-right turn into Sylvan Road. These few blocks of a suburban street represent a range of residential architecture and views of several old Queenslanders of the kind described by estate agents as 'ideal for the handyman' – a local euphemism for 'badly in need of restoration, but at least worthy of it'.

Historic Hotel

Ahead, beyond a railway overpass, the splendid old-Queensland-style three-storey **Regatta Hotel** marks your arrival at the riverside. Bear in mind as you admire the building that, in the course of Brisbane's worst floods in 1893, the water reached the top balcony.

The Regatta's other claim to fame arose from an incident in 1965 when it was still illegal for women to be served in a public bar in Queensland. Two rebellious and presumably thirsty young women managed to bring that rule into international ridicule by marching in, chaining themselves to the public bar and demanding to be served. The press had a field day photographing the offenders being set free with bolt-cutters, and the story, appearing in the national and international press, forced the embarrassed state government to repeal the law.

Depending on the time of day, you may care to un-chain yourself with a liberating XXXX before crossing Coronation Drive and heading for the combined

Top: red ginger blooms.
Left: lavender. **Right:** Oxley's on the River

walking and cycling track which takes you along the riverban to the city centre. About 3 metres (9½ft) wide, the paved path is marked with a centre line. Keep to the left, and the silent cyclists approaching from behind are obliged to give you right of way. If you want to cross the path for a closer view of the river, look behind you in case a cyclist is about to pass.

The river path is lower down the bank than the busy Coronation Drive, insulating you from traffic noise and offering vistas of a river populated by rowing teams (mostly at weekends), private craft and ferries. Much of the opposite bank is still protected as a mangrove habitat. The rowing clubs that are the source of much of the river's activity are located across from the Regatta Hotel on the river's Milton Reach. The vegetation along the path is a representative mixture of the native and the exotic.

River Rambles

Stop here and there, and enjoy the river scenery from one of the park benches along the route. If you've been walking slowly, you might appreciate an early lunch. About halfway between the Regatta and the city you'll come to **Oxley's on the River** (330 Coronation Drive; daily 11.30am–2.30pm; tel: 3368 1866), a pleasant restaurant built out over the water for wide views of the river and city. It's a good idea to book ahead, especially at weekends (or maybe bear it in mind for a scenic dinner at a later date). Otherwise, continue walking in the direction of your destination – and lunch – at the Riverside Centre. You'll enjoy the vistas of the city, framed by the arches of the Merivale and William Jolly bridges, along the pathway.

As you approach the city proper, your walking path runs underneath the elevated roadways where the traffic can be heard but not seen, still with views of the river and the opposite bank. Just after you pass under the Victoria Bridge, you'll see a ferry wharf area called Hayles Wharves. Look for some stone steps, ascend to street level and cross the bridge to the **South Bank Parkland**, your destination across the river. The afternoon section of our first Brisbane itinerary, *Getting to know Brisbane*, describes this multi-recreational area and some of its attractions (*see pages 23–24*).

6. Brisbane Ballooning *(see pull-out map)*

Get airborne at sunrise and survey the city from a bird's vantage point – drifting over the central business district and back over Brisbane suburbia; breakfast in style on terra firma.

A camera is a great asset on this four-hour excursion, and a zoom lens will enhance the variety of your pictures.

A hot-air balloon flight is an exciting and enchanting way to view Brisbane and its surroundings if you have some cash to spare. **Fly Me To The Moon Balloons** (tel: 3849 3185; www.flymetothemoon.com.au) picks you up at your hotel before sunrise, the actual time varying with the season between 4.30 and 5.30am. You will be driven to a meeting point where the crew, having reviewed the official weather and wind forecasts, then conduct their own micro-forecast by launching a small balloon and watching for indications of wind-shift as it ascends through the layers of air close to the ground. This helps them select a route (including the take-off and landing points) for skirting or flying over the Brisbane central business district and getting a series of down-the-chimney views of the city's suburbs. Balloon pilot Steve Griffin explains the crews' caution with the wry observation: 'The official weather forecasts are usually pretty accurate, it's just that sometimes they get the days mixed up.'

Pre-launch Preparation

The eight-passenger four-wheel drive, towing the balloon, basket and inflating equipment on a trailer, then takes you and your fellow-passengers to the selected launching point where the balloon is prepared, with some passenger participation in its unfurling and inflation. Pre-launch preparation takes around half an hour. The basket comes off the back of the trailer, followed by the balloon envelope, which has been carefully rolled up by the previous

Above: Brisbane seen from a balloon in the early morning

occupants. The crew's professionalism and confidence help passengers to relax. (Griffin, for example, is the holder of numerous ballooning records and has flown non-stop west to east across Australia.) Once in the traditional padded basket, you will receive a safety briefing before a few more jets of superheated air are fired into the huge envelope overhead. Levitating elegantly at about sunrise, your balloon drifts over Brisbane's serene and leafy outskirts. There is no advertised route for this aerial adventure because it depends on the winds of the day, but the path of your particular flight, which will have been selected before lift-off will most likely be west to east, originating somewhere to the southwest of Mount Coot-tha.

Bird's-Eye View

Your pilot gives a commentary on the parts of Brisbane that drift by underneath you, and there are of course wonderful photographic opportunities as the sun rises. Each flight is planned to fly close to, or directly above, Brisbane's business district, offering a leisurely bird's-eye view of this central area, which is enclosed on three sides by a giant loop in the Brisbane River. On the return journey, you drift back above residential suburbs. One aspect of Australian suburban life that becomes clear – if you haven't already observed it from the surface – is the 'quarter-acre block', the standard size chosen by many Australians as the minimum lot size on which to build a family-sized home.

You should also gain an insight into how a balloon is navigated – by varying its height to capture the wind shifts at different levels. These wind changes are exploited with great skill to achieve a smooth approach and landing in soft grass, where your ground crewman, confident of the navigational outcome, will be already waiting with his vehicle. Passengers with cameras are invited to disembark to photograph the still-inflated balloon.

Flight duration varies according to prevailing climatic conditions, but 50 minutes to one hour is about the average. Deflating and re-packing is a communal activity in which you will be invited to participate. For this you are well rewarded: your four-wheel-drive vehicle stops at a pretty public park, you're invited to sit at a table, and a substantia gourmet breakfast materialises, along with ample champagne to stretch out the exhilaration you're already feeling from your flight.

The ballooning company will drive you to your hotel, where you'll arrive about four hours after pickup, leaving you either to catch up on your sleep or to move on to another of our itineraries.

Right: gone with the wind

7. Wildlife Wonders *(see pull-out map)*

Cruise up the Brisbane River to Lone Pine Sanctuary to cuddle a koala; look out also for kangaroos, wallabies, dingos and wombats.

This half-day excursion can be shortened by using a taxi or bus instead of our recommended mode of transport; and it can be made to fit other itineraries with a bit of planning – in particular, a walk from Mount Coot-tha to the city or the Queensland Woolshed visit.

It has become almost mandatory for overseas visitors to be photographed cuddling a koala, perhaps because these winsome creatures are featured on so many tourist brochures. The koala's natural habitat is the eucalyptus forests of eastern and southeastern Australia, and it is most at home in south-eastern Queensland. Its popularity is deserved and you should definitely make the time to include an encounter with the marsupial on your itinerary.

Of the various opportunities you will have to socialise with koalas, a visit to the **Lone Pine Sanctuary** (tel: 3378 1366; www.koala.net) is your best bet. On an upstream loop of the Brisbane River, Lone Pine can be reached by taxi or bus. Better still, at least in one direction, take a leisurely and scenic 19-km (12-mile) cruise up the Brisbane River on *Mirimar* (tel: 3221 0300), a stately, 60-year-old timber vessel that departs daily at 10am from North Quay at the top of Queen Street Mall. Included on the voyage is a well-researched and entertaining commentary on contemporary and historical Brisbane. Anecdotes abound about the owners – and the sometimes sinister history – of the riverbank's stately homes. (Brisbane's citizens often speculate on the reasons why anybody would want to live along the riverbank at all, given that in the big flood in 1974, some 18,000 homes were, for a time, submerged under the muddy floodwaters.) While you listen to the intermittent commentary, you can take advantage of the tea and coffee on offer.

You should arrive at Lone Pine's private jetty at **Fig Tree Pocket** at about 11.20am. This will give you plenty of time to enjoy the sanctuary before returning on *Mirimar* (departing 2.30pm and arriving North Quay 3.50pm). If you want to stay longer, check the bus timetable in advance.

Marsupials Galore

First of all, get this right. Although koalas look a bit like bears and are often called 'koala bears', in fact they're not bears at all. Like many of Australia's native animals, such as kangaroos and wallabies, they're marsupials, which means that the baby lives in its mother's pouch for a period after its birth – in the case of koalas, for around five to six months. The young koala then rides on his mother's back for another six months or so. Weaning is complete by the time the koala is a year old, after which it will exist almost

Above: a pretty-face wallaby protects her offspring at Lone Pine Sanctuary
Top Right: a dingo, Australia's native dog. **Right:** a Lone Pine koala takes a lunch break

exclusively on the foliage of a handful of the country's 700-odd species of eucalyptus tree.

Koalas are most active just after sunset. They sleep for about 18 hours a day and don't drink much water, but they are voracious eaters. The sanctuary maintains a substantial plantation of eucalyptus trees to ensure a guaranteed supply of food. Furthermore, Lone Pine goes to great lengths to keep its koalas in natural surroundings and to limit the amount of stress induced by tourists who, for example, can't resist a cuddle. For that reason, there's a 'roster' to limit the human interaction experienced by the animals. If you haven't brought your camera with you, Lone Pine provides a koala-cuddling photo-service with same-day processing and return.

Native Fauna

Although they are undoubtedly the star attraction, koalas share Lone Pine with a wealth of fellow indigenous creatures, including a fine range of kangaroo and wallaby species, some of which are relatively rare. These include the agile wallaby, the common wallaroo, the eastern grey kangaroo, the pretty-face wallaby, the red kangaroo of the arid regions, the red-legged pademelon, the red-necked wallaby, the rufous bettong and the swamp wallaby. You should also be able to see the dingo (a native dog found in many areas across Australia), the wombat, which is a close relation of the koala, and a vast representation of bats, reptiles, birds and amphibians. The sanctuary staff are friendly, patient and well-informed, promoting a good understanding of the country's indigenous fauna.

8. Rural Heritage (see pull-out map)

To witness life in the bush the easy way, visit the Australian Woolshed by train; watch a show that includes wool-spinning techniques; treat yourself to a 'billy tea and damper' session.

The price of wool was falling, in eighteen ninety-one.
The men who owned the acres saw something must be done.
'We will break the shearers' union, and show we're masters still,
And they'll take the terms we give them, or we'll find the men who will.'
[Outback folk song]

In the event, it didn't work out that way, and the squatters' intransigence led to the formation of Australia's first trade union. The grit and determination of the country's outback pioneers, many of them newly-liberated convicts or their descendants, thrust them into two camps: the landholders, including the unauthorised but usually unchallenged land squatters who had actually obtained the titles to (or control of) land, and the workers who didn't care to be pushed around. This division nearly brought civil war to the bush. The spirit of independence that still impels some Australians to 'go bush', where the work is harder and the rewards less readily obtained, remains a powerful component of the modern Australian psyche.

Sheepish Activities

Much of the bush is a long way inland, and it isn't exactly full of attractive and interesting features anyway. But if you want to sample some bush highlights, check out

Above: going with the herd
Left: surrogate mum

the **Australian Woolshed** (148 Samford Road, Ferny Hills; shows: 8am, 9.30am, 11am, 1pm and 2.30pm; tel: 3351 5366; www.auswoolshed.com.au). The Woolshed manages to evoke a credible simulation of life on a typical outback sheep station.

The Australian Woolshed in Brisbane is only 14km (9 miles) from the centre of the city. Trains to Ferny Grove station leave at regular intervals from Brisbane Central. From Ferny Grove, the Woolshed is a short, pleasant stroll away. From Saturdays to Wednesdays, if given 24 hours' notice, the Woolshed can arrange to collect you from Ferny Grove station in an authentic old-style horse and cart and deposit you right outside its entrance.

Shear Torture

Every Woolshed show features a sheep-shearing demonstration. Beyond its entertainment value, this will help the visitor to understand, among other things, why shearers often have to retire early with back problems; and if you can imagine shearing more than 100 sheep a day in the stultifying heat of the outback, you will realise why shearers have earned an awesome reputation for downing large numbers of after-work beers in record time. There are also sheepdog trials in which the sheepdogs, encouraged by their owners, seem intent on playing to the audience rather than focusing on the task of rounding up reluctant sheep.

Other highlights include displays of bush arts such as stockwhip cracking, and simple demonstrations of wool spinning given by the Woolshed's resident spinner. The Woolshed Ram Show delineates and compares the various breeds of sheep. If you wish, you can try hand-feeding a lamb or calf or milking a cow. The Ram Show also offers the opportunity to hear the didgeridoo, an Aboriginal musical instrument that looks like a massive, wooden clarinet. It's actually a long piece of hollowed-out wood decorated with Aboriginal art.

Every Ram Show session features the telling of yarns about Australia's colourful past. Given that Australians are at their best when expressing their sardonic, self-mocking sense of humour, you shouldn't miss this quirky narrative. And if bush poetry sounds like a contradiction in terms, hear a recital to be proved wrong. One of the most traditional re-enactments is the 'billy tea and damper' session. (A billy is a converted tin of the preserved-fruit variety; a damper is a kind of bush bread baked, without yeast, in the coals of a campfire.) It's worth scheduling your visit to the Woolshed to be there for a hearty country breakfast (7.30–10.30am) or a big barbecue lunch (10.30am–3.30pm), which can include barbecued kangaroo, or prime rib fillet of beef at modest prices. Woolshed Ram Show translation sheets are available in Chinese, Japanese, Thai, Korean and Indonesian.

Right: a billy tea and damper

The Gold Coast

The Gold Coast prides itself on ensuring that all its people – residents and visitors alike – enjoy themselves. The very fact that its collective daily goal is the total entertainment of everybody who's there on that particular day (or night) means that some of its offerings will not suit the individual's personal tastes. However, the creators of one of the world's most diverse range of attractions offer the promise that as long as your preferences are legal, it's very unlikely that you'll be disappointed.

The garishness that characterises the high-rise section of The Strip, culminating in Surfers Paradise (*see page 51*), Queensland's answer to Ipanema, Miami and Cannes, diminishes the further you travel along the coast. Along those 57km (35 miles) of magnificent ocean beach, there are places so far away from the glitz that you can imagine that you're entirely alone. Low-rise apartments and hotels take the place of the high-rise establishments, inexpensive family-style motels offer affordable accommodation and low-cost eateries compete for your business without sacrificing quality.

Against that background, let's look at a small selection of the attractions offered by The Coast.

9. The Heart of the Coast *(see map, p51)*

Tour the Coast by Aquabus taking in Sea World and canal-development residences; lunch at a surf club; visit Currumbin Wildlife Sanctuary; go shopping before dinner.

The Aquabus operates from 10am every 75 minutes. It is often fully booked, so make a reservation by telephone well in advance (tel: 5539 0222; www.aquabus.com.au).

It was the surf that first lured people to the beaches, and it's the surf that is still the prime attraction. The freshness of an early-morning amble on the beach attracts residents and visitors of all ages. Your accommodation is likely to be within rumbling distance of the surf, so take some shoes that are suitable for negotiating the sand (or that are easy to take off) and spend an hour or so enjoying the Coast's prime non-manufactured form of entertainment.

If the weather's favourable, remember to take swimwear and a towel along with you. Though Australians aren't exactly famous for their modesty, you won't have to change in public – there are plenty of clean and well-maintained changing rooms. When swimming, you must keep to the area between the flags; if there aren't any flags, it means that there are no lifeguards on duty, so don't swim at all. Pre-breakfast is a good time to take a dip,

Left: a great way to explore
Right: summer fun on the Gold Coast

but if you prefer to hit the beach later and the sun is bright, apply plenty of sunscreen and wear a hat. If this seems trivial, you should be aware that melanoma (skin cancer) is common among Queensland's longer-term residents.

Surf Crazy

In the early-morning sun, the terraced towers provide a striking contrast with the primeval power of the ocean. If the surf's up, as it almost always is on the Gold Coast, surfing's international brigade of youthful devotees will be riding the waves from dawn. **Main Beach** at the northern end of the high-rises is particularly popular with the surfies, but you'll find them performing almost everywhere along the strip. The row of yellow elevated observation boxes are there as lookout towers for the lifeguards, who regularly perform serious rescues even on the mildest days. The towers provide an ever-present reminder to respect the rules of beach safety, the most important of which is never to swim outside the flags.

Your walk can start anywhere and finish anywhere – the beach is almost continuous long the entire Gold Coast. Such early-morning exertions are bound to give you a healthy appetite, so you will probably appreciate a good breakfast. Wherever there is holiday accommodation in the vicinity, restaurants are ready to compete for your custom with bargain breakfasts, whether coffee and doughnuts or substantial American-style affairs.

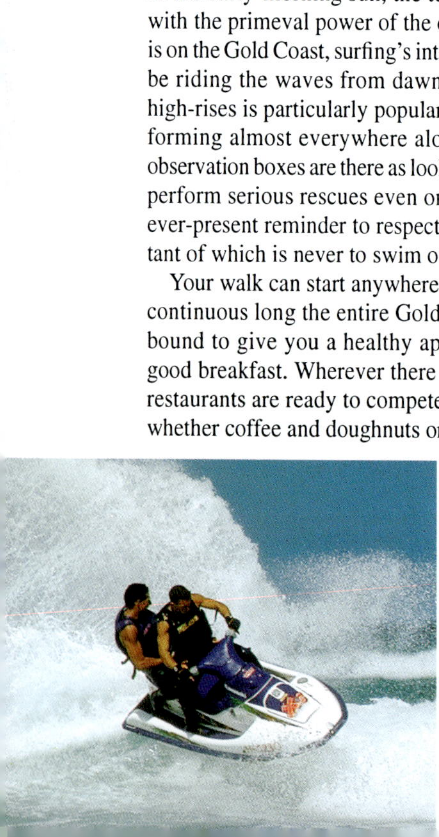

Aquabus Tours

After breakfast, there's no more original way to acquire your first overview of the Gold Coast than by **Aquabus Safaris** (tel: 5539 0222; www.aquabus.com.au), an innovative and popular city-sights guided tour on an amphibious vehicle. Book an early trip – preferably the first of the day

Above: joining an Aquabus Safari
Left: jet ski in action

at 10am – at least a day ahead. You realise that this odd-looking vehicle isn't a run-of-the-mill bus when you board it at a central pickup point by climbing in over the side via a gangway with a rope rail. The open-sided Aquabus, which has room for 34 passengers, trundles northwards along the coastal esplanade, sounding like a well-used ferryboat, towards the extremities of the Southport Spit. The crew uses a PA system to brief passengers on the area's development and its highlights, including **Sea World** (*see page 65*). The bus heads towards the road's northern end and, as it runs out of road, descends down a ramp and plunges into the well-sheltered Broadwater. Transformed into a slow boat, it backtracks down the Gold Coast waterways to provide an interesting new perspective on the region for anyone who has seen it only from the land.

While the Aquabus chugs under a bridge, passing the opulent residences of the canal-development area, you are treated to a colourful commentary on the Coast's history, its heroes and villains, and its prime real estate. It eventually lurches ashore and delivers passengers back to its city terminal. If you took the 10am trip, your amphibious escapade will have landed you back in the epicentre of **Surfers Paradise**'s shopping precinct before most shoppers have surfaced, so it's a good time to stock up on souvenirs and gifts or at least check out the land for a return trip.

Indigenous Products

The stores stock the big international brand labels as well as the Coast's own array of merchandise. Although some Australiana products such as local clothing, ornaments, artistic prints and Aboriginal didgeridoos are genuine, some are produced in Asian countries, so if you want an authentic indigenous product, look for the distinctive Australian-made labels. A section of the Coast's retailing industry feels obliged to live up to its tacky reputation, and in their own self-mocking way, some shopkeepers have elevated bad taste to an art-form: T-shirts are prime banners for tongue-in-cheek expressions of new-found personal philosophies. (*See Shopping, page 69,* for more details.)

Lunch at a Surf Club

Wherever you are along the Coast, you're rarely more than a few hundred metres/yards from one of the 30-odd surf lifesaving clubs (around 25 of which have restaurants or cafés, half of them licensed). There was a time when surfing was illegal. Victorian morality deemed the human form as displayed in a bathing costume indecent, and public bathing was permitted only after nightfall, and even then the genders were kept strictly segregated. But as the new age of the 20th century dawned, surfing was gaining more and more adherents. In 1902, a determined group of surfers at Sydney's Manly Beach defied the law and, wearing neck-to-knee swimwear, launched themselves into the waves in broad daylight.

As the sport took off, its popularity forced a change in the laws and experienced surfers were able to form small local lifesaving groups to help in rescues, and to develop lifesaving techniques. The first such club in Queens-

land opened on Coolangatta Beach, and today approximately 80,000 members belong to some 300 lifesaving clubs nationwide.

The Australian National Lifesaving contests attract thousands of competitors from clubs in every state, and a vast number of spectators. One third of the clubs' members are women, and the proportion is growing. Competitions are held most frequently during the summer months, from around mid-September to the end of April, during which time surf-club volunteers patrol the beaches. During the remainder of the year, the beaches are watched by local-government lifeguards, who are frequently called upon to perform rescues (around 2,800 rescues per season off Queensland's beaches) There's every possibility that, during your stay, a competitive event, or at least a training session, will take place on a beach near you. For information on contests, call the Queensland Surf Lifesaving Association (tel: 3846 8000, office hours; www.lifesaving.com.au). The association publishes a calendar of events.

The lifesaving clubs are situated on prime beach-front land, usually with a fine view of the surf, and almost all of them serve generous informal lunches and good-quality dinners at modest prices, though don't expect waitress service. You must sign the visitors' book to gain admission, but the locals are friendly and just about anyone will sign you in if you announce yourself as a visitor to the region. The location of the clubs is usually marked by a yellow lifeguard tower. At those clubs that have more than one tower, ask a lifeguard to direct you to the clubhouse. Dining times vary between clubs and seasons, but most are around 12 noon–2pm for lunch and 7pm onwards for dinner.

If you decide to take a turn on the club's gaming machines, it's even more important that you have signed in; the Queensland Liquor Act stipulates that you can claim your winnings only if your name is in the visitors' book and you come from more than 40km (25 miles) away.

Back to Nature

After lunch, you may want to take in something entirely different: **Currumbin Wildlife Sanctuary** (daily 8am–5pm; tel: 5598 1645; www.currumbin-sanctuary.org.au). If you haven't hired your own car, get there by taxi or bus. Surfside bus lines will never keep you waiting more than about 15 minutes at their terminal at the Dolphin Arcade, near the corner of Cavill Avenue and the Gold Coast Highway, or at any bus stop along the route. Take a 1 or 1A bus or, if you are driving, look out for the brown signs to the sanctuary, which is situated a couple of kilometres (1 mile) north of Coolangatta airport.

Founded in 1947 by an enthusiastic beekeeper, Alex Griffiths, this appealing wildlife sanctuary is now home to more than 1,600 native Australian birds and animals. Many of these creatures were brought to the sanctuary after being injured by traffic or predators, be they animal or human. Most have been, one way or another, victims of 'progress'.

Top Left: Paradise city centre
Left: lifesavers compete. **Right:** a Black Mountain Possum

Rainbow Lorikeet

The rainbow lorikeet is one of the wildlife sanctuary's foremost attractions. Griffiths began hand-feeding these chattering, gregarious, multi-hued parrots, which arrive in flocks of untold numbers, years ago. The idea was to divert them from plundering his favourite cultivated flowers, which they would attack in search of nectar. The birds became such a popular attraction that Griffiths decided to establish the sanctuary around them. After buying up the neighbouring land to increase the size of his project, Griffiths donated the sanctuary to the National Trust. Today Currumbin is a peaceful haven amidst the Gold Coast's surfeit of artificial splendours and excesses.

Be at Currumbin no later than 3.30pm, when a group of Aborigines from a tribe on South Stradbroke Island presents the *Nunukul Kunjeil.* This folkloric performance of tribal dancing incorporates Aboriginal myths and legends – and a display of traditional firefighting methods – accompanied by the deep rumble of the didgeridoo. Immediately afterwards you have an opportunity to participate in feeding the squawking lorikeets, which flock to the sanctuary in time for 8am and 4pm daily feeding sessions. These birds are far from being domesticated, so wear easily-washable clothing and a broad-brimmed hat – a form of protection adopted by the attendants.

By around 5pm the crowds on the beach will have drifted back to the bars, the bistros and the multi-ethnic, alfresco licensed eateries along The Strip and around the shopping malls. Everywhere locals and visitors will be re-grouping to make the most of the evening ahead over a cold green can of the ubiquitous Fosters or a technicolour cocktail. In the latter category, you might want to try a Dingo's Blood, a Tropical Itch or a Mango Tango.

If the rowdy *après*-surf scene doesn't appeal, you could sit on your balcony watching the sunset's rich colours fade while planning your evening (*see pages 76–77*). It's still far too early to take refuge in sleep.

Top: Currumbin Sanctuary
Right: Aboriginal dance

10. Gold Coast Scenic Rim *(see map, p51)*

Hire a car and savour the scenic splendour of Eagle Heights and Mount Tamborine; continue to Binna Burra Mountain Lodge; walk the Rainforest Circuit; have lunch at the Binna Burra Lodge or Lamington Tea House; enjoy more scenery by car or on foot.

You will need a self-drive car and fine, sunny weather to enjoy a relaxing day, because low cloud around the hills spoils the views, renders the rainforests soggy and makes driving far less of a pleasure.

While on the beach, you might have looked over your shoulder and noticed the range of mountains that form the Gold Coast's backdrop. Today, 'go bush' to explore 'the green behind the gold' (the national colours), which represents at least a few of the broad range of rural and wilderness environments that blend into a diverse and ever-changing rural Australia. This is a whole-day tour. If you're particularly taken by the multitude of large and small national parks, you might want to spend a whole day amidst the scenic splendour of **Eagle Heights and Mount Tamborine**. Should you choose this option, return to the coast via Canungra and the scenic Coomera Gorge road. If, however, you continue to **Binna Burra** but decide to undertake one of the longer walks, you can return direct to the coast via Nerang, maybe even returning to resume your trip the following day. A third alternative is to do the full circuit with shorter stops.

Mount Tamborine

To leave the coastal strip and embark on your trip as fast as possible, take the quickest inland route to intercept the Gold Coast Highway, joining it at or before Nerang (depending on where exactly on the strip you're staying). Drive north to Oxenford, passing the big theme parks before turning off and following the signs to Tamborine. If you have responsible teenage children whose absence will make for an even more peaceful day's driving, you could leave them at one of the three theme parks (*see page 65–7*) and

Above: looking over Numinbah Valley

collect them at the end of the day. It's usually a good idea to meet at a precise point near the entrance to one of the attractions. Alternatively, if they're up for an adventure on public transport, provide them with the bus fare back to the Coast and reunite there.

Take the Mount Tamborine road at Oxenford and follow it for about 2 km (just over a mile) before turning right on a route that takes inexorably to the hills. The winding road ascends through a mixture of native bush and rolling foothills to **Eagle Heights** (average 500 metres/1,630ft above sea level), where you may find yourself dreaming of living in one of the elegant residences that command sweeping views of the Gold Coast, its hinterland and the ocean beyond. (Don't be confused by the geographical curiosity which locates North Tamborine south of Tamborine.) Another oddity is that the whole of this area – Eagle Heights, North Tamborine and Mount Tamborine – is known collectively as Mount Tamborine.

Teas and Tarts

The diversity of the craft shops and eateries is not the result of cynical efforts to exploit the tourist boom but rather reflects the multinational origins of the residents. Examples include Café Amore, Chef Jacques' Sidewalk Restaurant, The Polish Place, Dutch Clog Workshop, and Swedish Corner. The majority of the area's small national parks feature a variety of forest types and incorporate unusually diverse blends of native palms, eucalypts, ancient cedars, beeches and figs. Get a free local map from the visitors' information centre to help you identify which parks are which. By now your botanical browsing and souvenir scanning will have brought the time close to 10am, the official opening time for 'teas and tarts' at most of the teahouses and restaurants, galleries and craft shops.

Two delightful morning-tea options are highly recommended. For the first, take a right turn at the roundabout just beyond Eagle Heights, pass the Fuchsia Farm (on the left) and after a two-minute drive you'll reach the **Pavilion Gardens Restaurant & Crafts** (10am–4pm) where you can enjoy your mid-morning refreshments in a rainforest milieu surrounded by lots of native birdlife. Alternatively, continue along the same road through the attractive bushland, which features tall palms and spreading rainforest trees, and take the first left until you reach **Main Street Café** in **North Tamborine**. The Devonshire teas that are the speciality here are complemented by an 'olde English' setting and indeed the proprietors' accents. The café is close to the centre of a quaint country-town shopping area which has succeeded in preserving its old-style character.

With its beautiful national parks and its art galleries, coffee houses, village gardens and craft shops, Mount Tamborine might well detain you all day. When you've eventually had enough and it's time to return to base, take

Above: Maine Street Café serves English-style cream teas
Top Right: Welcome to Lamington National Park. **Right:** braille on the Senses Trail

the Tamborine Mountain road to Mount Tamborine proper, then the Tamborine-Nerang road. Use a low gear on the steep descent to save your brakes. (This route will return you to any kids you may have left at the theme parks.)

If you're still on schedule, however, continue past Mount Tamborine towards Canungra, again in low gear when descending what is known as the Goat Track. Turn left when you reach the Canungra-Nerang crossroads and right about 4km (2 miles) further on at the sign for the Beechmont/Binna Burra road. You've descended into the Coomera River Valley, and are now climbing the opposite ridge to Beechmont, where you'll enjoy more views of the hinterland, the Nerang River Valley and the Coast. Turn right at the hilltop village of Beechmont for a 10-km (6-mile) drive to **Binna Burra Mountain Lodge**, 800 metres (2,600ft) above sea level, in the World Heritage-listed, 20,000-hectare (50,000-acre) **Lamington National Park**. Binna Burra, which has been in operation since the 1930s, was the first resort in the region to gain official eco-tourism accreditation. By the time you reach Binna Burra, you'll have driven (depending on your starting point and any detours) approximately 90km (56 miles). The National Parks & Wildlife Service information centre just before Binna Burra is not always staffed, but it does display maps.

Ornithology

Birdwatching is popular among keen amateurs and serious 'twitchers'. There are quite a number of common species that are unique to this region and, with the help of an ornithology guide, you may identify whipbirds, green catbirds or lyre-birds. You might also see or hear the rarer species such as the paradise rifle bird or the rufous scrub bird. If you don't fancy a long trek, you should follow at least one of Binna Burra's briefer recommended walks to

see what the park has to offer. Ask at the lodge's reception desk for more detailed information about the various trails.

The 500-metre/yard long **Senses Trail** gives sight-impaired visitors the opportunity to experience the natural wonderland that surrounds them through the use of guide ropes and braille signs. Sighted visitors are encouraged to don blindfolds to heighten the awareness of their senses. About 20 minutes, or 1.2km (¾ mile) away is the **Rainforest Circuit.** Follow the Border Track for 500 metres/yards, then branch right and return to the picnic area. Get a guide leaflet from the information centre, campground kiosk or Binna Burra Lodge to help you navigate this short walk. Another short-walk option is the **Bellbird Lookout walk.** This track branches off the Ships Stern Circuit and descends into rainforest and open-forest terrain before emerging at the Lookout. The 2km (just over a mile) return walk rewards you with excellent views of towering rocky bluffs and the Numinbah Valley. The valley used to be the forest habitat of the valuable hoop pine and the red cedar, the harvesting of which led to the establishment of the first European settlement here, which in turn ultimately resulted in the clearing of the valley.

Lunchtime Views

You have two choices for lunch: one is the Lodge's clifftop dining room, which has sweeping views of the Beechmont Plateau and Coomera Valley, and a rustic ambience. The Lodge's hearty home-style meals with a salad buffet and a selection of hot dishes should satiate your appetite. And its

community dining gives you the opportunity to socialise with the dedicated and knowledgeable bushwalkers who make up Binna Burra's core clientele. Lunch is traditionally signalled by a ship's bell at 1pm sharp. It's advisable to book (tel: 1800 074260; www.binnaburralodge.com.au). If the walk hasn't left you ravenous, the other lunch option, for which booking is unnecessary, is the Lamington Tea House (open Mon–Fri 8am–5pm, Sat–Sun 8am–8pm), adjacent to the camping ground. As its name suggests, the Tea House serves light meals and snacks. The children's adventure playground nearby is designed to help the young to experience and comprehend rainforest ecosystems.

If, after lunch, you want to take one of Binna Burra's longer walks and spend the rest of the day there, you should take the Beechmont and Nerang route back to the Coast. The drive will probably take less than an hour.

Spoilt for Choice

The multitude of variables in this itinerary reflect the large array of options. If you have allowed yourself the time, take the same route from Binna Burra, the Nerang Road, through lower Beechmont, but turn right close to the bottom of the hill and take the Nerang-Murwillumbah road. This takes you up the scenic **Numinbah Valley** to the national park named after the **Natural Arch**, the park's main attraction. The pleasant drive through the Numinbah State Forest's natural bushland takes you through virtually unpopulated country. About 30km (18 miles) from the Advancetown turn-off, and off a well-signed side road to the left, you will find the **Natural Arch café-restaurant** (10am–5pm daily, closed Mon; tel: 5533 6140) at the car park for the Natural Arch (also known as the Natural Bridge) itself. A one-kilometre (half-mile) circular walk brings you to this peculiar formation where the **Cave Creek** stream plunges through the eroded roof of an underground basalt cavern. You can enter further down the pathway to view the resulting waterfall. From here you can see how the cavern's exit forms a near-perfect archway through which the creek leaves the cave.

To take the recommended route back to the Gold Coast, continue further south on the same very scenic road. The 30km (18 miles) to Murwillumbah passes through a gap in the hills with fine views of **Mount Warning**, the 22 million-year-old, now-extinct core of Australia's biggest volcano, which was named by Captain Cook. The road winds down to the Tweed Valley through alternating lush, hilly farmland and rich, subtropical rainforest, with Mount Warning towering beyond. The road crosses the border into New South Wales, passing sugar-cane and banana plantations and the Condon sugar mill beside the wide, sweeping Tweed River, as you turn north along the main highway for the quick run back to the Gold Coast.

Top Left: sounding the lunch bell at Binna Burra Lodge
Left: Cave Creek. **Right:** picnic with Mount Warning as a backdrop

11. A South Sea Island Cruise *(see pull-out map)*

Test your aquatic skills (no previous experience required) en route to McLarens Landing; understand how it feels to be a seagull; enjoy a barbecue lunch at The Homestead; swim and relax.

There are optional add-ons during this rather unstructured aquatic tour, but its core is a peaceful cruise on calm, clear waters at an unhurried pace.

'Slip on a shirt, slop on some sunscreen and slap on a hat.' This slogan, taken from Queensland TV's well-publicised public-health promotion, is admirable advice for today's voyage, even though there's plenty of shade aboard the good ships ***Maranoa*** and ***Sir Henry Morgan***, named after a 17th-century British buccaneer of long-debated reputation. The 25-metre (84-ft) barquentine (a sailing ship of three or more masts rigged square on the foremast and fore-and-aft on the others), carries a maximum of 60 passengers and leaves the Marina Mirage at 9am for a leisurely sail through the Broadwater's sparkling shallows. **Tall Ship Sailing Cruises** (tel: 5532 2444; www.tallship.com.au) offers a full-day, steak-and-seafood adventure cruise that docks at two of the islands. There's free all-day parking at Marina Mirage or, alternatively, a free pickup from most accommodation houses. Remember to bring your swimwear, because there will almost certainly be opportunities for a swim, or snorkelling, in the calm waters at **McLarens Landing** on the pristine, all-sand **South Stradbroke Island**, your noontime stopover destination.

Cardboard Cutlasses

At least some of the six-member crew are likely to be members of the proprietor's family; the remainder only act like family. Your voyage begins with a safety briefing, after which the natural-born clowns among the crew will help

Top: an adventure cruise on a Tall Ship
Above: a ship's throttle

you to relax. Don't jump overboard, for example, if you're confronted by a piratical-looking villain waving a cutlass. The cutlasses are made of cardboard, and the same blackguard may soon be making your morning tea. The ship sails up the Broadwater 'under canvas', but is assisted by engine power when the wind isn't cooperating. You will doubtlessly notice the attendant 'bumboats', whose wares are enthusiastically promoted by the crew.

Although you haven't yet had a chance to become bored (and won't), you will be offered, at a moderate add-on price, the chance to supplement the day's experience while your vessel sails serenely northward. First comes the option of para-sailing, which requires no skill or training. If you don't like heights but do appreciate thrills, Crazy Dave offers the alternative of a wild speedboat ride on the usually calm waters. If this doesn't appeal, how about a quick scenic flight aboard a seaplane? Hop into a bumboat, then climb aboard the seaplane, and within minutes you're enjoying a panoramic aerial view of the Gold Coast, its surroundings and attractions.

Artificial Lagoon

In the course of all these activities, you're getting closer to the **Sanctuary Cove** canal estate. This estate is a classic example of the triumph of progress over marshland. Indeed the controversial development led Queensland's high-rolling estate agents to be dubbed the 'White Shoe Brigade' (a term that referred to slick property developers from the southern states, who tended to dress in what they perceived to be the garb of a subtropical businessman). Under-utilised pleasure-craft worth millions of dollars lap gently at the marinas' waters. Docking here, you will have the opportunity to shop at the resort-style boutiques whose wares, though expensive, tend to be of good quality. You might speculate on the whereabouts of the residents of the opulent but seemingly deserted and rather uniform-looking dwellings around the artificial lagoon. Perhaps they're playing golf on one of the nearby courses, or are busy running their businesses in the Deep South. For a 'before and after' view of the development, look across the watercourse at the mangroves, which retain their state of raw wilderness.

The actual route of your short crossing to **The Homestead**, a truly serene location at **McLarens Landing**, now depends on the state of the tide. At the end of the jetty, you will be welcomed by the staff of The Homestead, a low-key day resort in an open-air, breezy bush setting. Equally welcoming are the scents of a good old Aussie barbecue, and – as everywhere else – a licensed bar. Inclusive lunch options include oversized eye-fillet or large T-bone steaks, chicken teriyaki and similar temptations, with a side-salad. The 'barbie' is filling to say the least, and the location is so close to nature you're likely to be visited by an unusually charming marsupial, the golden swamp wallaby, which will doubtlessly be hoping to share your meal. It's bad for indigenous animals to eat anything other than their regular diet, so don't succumb to their charms.

Right: ready to peel

After lunch, you might want to swim and sunbathe on the lovely expanse of beach; you might want to try jet-skiing, pedal-boating or water-skiing, or you might decide to take a fully-guided tour of the wilderness in an air-conditioned, four-wheel-drive coach. If you take this last option, you'll cross South Stradbroke Island on the way to the ocean-facing beach, bumping, though not too uncomfortably, through the forested sandhills. These are populated by kangaroo and wallaby herds, flocks of native birds and other Australian wildlife. Don't expect to swim in the ocean here. The beach isn't patrolled, and the water has dangerous tidal rips, to say nothing of the odd shark. None of these dangers apply to swimming on the Broadwater side at McLarens Landing.

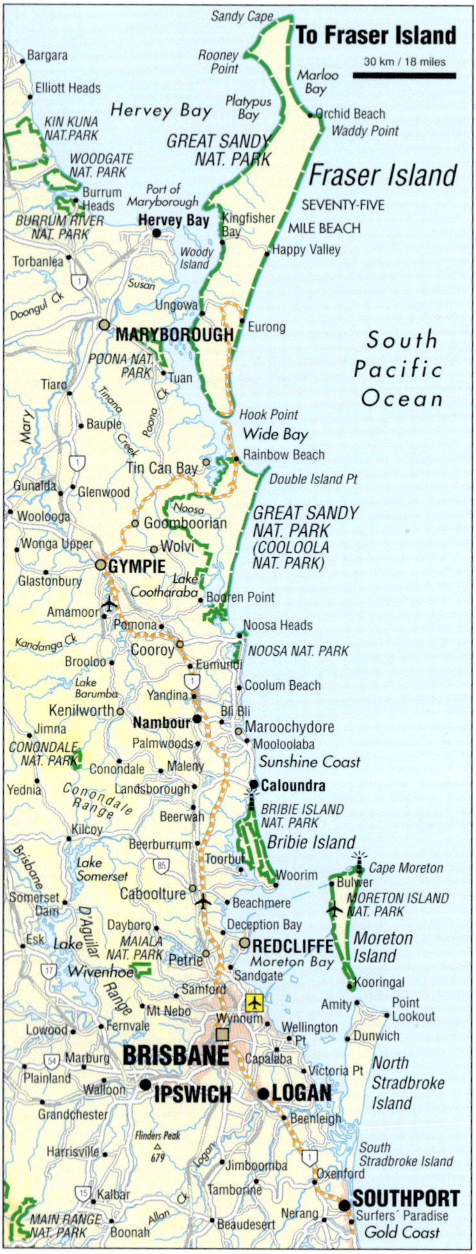

You leave for the return voyage at about 2.30pm, but timekeeping in this relaxed environment is conducted with less precision than you may be accustomed to. The journey back might take up to two hours, but by this stage you're bound to be feeling relaxed and reluctant to end the trip. The crew now starts piling on the entertainment, and the yacht, clearly designed for luxury cruising, offers ample below-deck space for the less energetic to sit and chat over a drink, or take a nap.

Para-sailing

On the way back there's also the option of discounted para-sailing, which is great fun, and not nearly as scary as it might first appear. Expect to be back at Marina Mirage by around 4.30pm. Alternatively, if you're seduced by the serenity of The Homestead and its surroundings (including an hospitable resort lying just a few hundred metres/yards south along the beach), you can stay for a couple of hours longer and be ferried by water taxi back to your starting point at no additional charge.

12. Fraser Island *(see map, p62)*

Venture into the wilderness to visit Fraser Island; take swimwear; explore Wanggoolba Creek rainforest; drive on the beach; have dinner at the Rainbow Beach Hotel or the Surf Lifesaving Club.

This is a long but rewarding day, which can also be undertaken from Brisbane.

'The world's most beautiful highway.' That distinction belongs not to a conventional thoroughfare, but to a 120-km (75-mile) stretch of surf-washed golden beach without signposts, traffic lights, petrol stations – or even a proper surface. Whether travelling from Brisbane or the Gold Coast, a sortie a little further afield offers a unique wilderness experience, which is really saying something because there's a lot of wilderness in Australia. Hidden among the offerings of **Australian Day Tours** (tel: 1300 363436, operating Tues, Thurs, Sat; www.daytours.com.au) is an opportunity to visit **Fraser Island**, the world's largest sand island. As befits a wilderness, it takes some time to reach and makes for rather a long day. If you'd like to spend more time on the island than is allotted in this excursion, you can travel there on a Tuesday, stay two nights at **Eurong Resort** on the ocean-facing beach, and return on the Thursday.

Coastal Bushland

Pickup by coach from your Gold Coast accommodation is at or about 6.30am to allow for the hour's drive to Brisbane to pick up passengers there. Have an early breakfast or take some refreshments with you, because your first stop is not until **Matildas** near Gympie. The next hour's drive is through natural coastal bushland typical of the area's sandy wetlands. This is an introduction to the kind of wilderness you're approaching. At **Rainbow Beach** you'll find a lovely village which looks like a fishing village without the fishing.

Here, you transfer to a 40-seat, air-conditioned four-wheel drive bus, purpose-built for the task ahead, which takes you to the vehicular ferry. Your knowledgeable guide joins you for the day. After a 10-minute drive,

Above: Fraser Island

you're aboard the ferry to Fraser Island, where you arrive at its southernmost tip and cross an enigmatic rainforest environment featuring white silicon sand, and freshwater 'perched lakes' (so-called because they are above sea level, and are fed by the slow filtering of rainwater through the sand of the surrounding dunes, which makes their waters crystal clear). The lakes move with the sand; should you come back next year you will discover that the lake has shifted some 10cm (3 ins) to the northwest on the prevailing winds as the sand fills in the windward side and the wavelets scallop out the other side. Mineral sand mining and wholesale logging, once major industries here, were halted some years ago in an attempt to help the island revert to its natural state. Eurong, a lovely resort above the beach, is the northern-most point you'll visit in the six hours or so that you spend on the island, and you can enjoy a good lunch there.

Virgin Rainforest

One of the day's highlights is a stop at one of the creeks that flow through the outstanding rainforest areas on this lovely island. Here the beautiful crystal-clear stream runs through virgin rainforest. Birds flutter through the treetops, which are self-contained ecosystems that support a diverse botanical collection of orchids, ferns, and vines. If the tide is high, its quite possible that the bus will get stuck in the mud. When this happens, the passengers get out, not only to lighten the load, but in the case of the fit and strong to provide some pushing power, until the stricken vehicle is freed. If the situation requires more drastic action, a rescue vehicle based at Eurong will come to your assistance. The beach scenery takes on a new dimension when seen from a vehicle. The coloured dunes of mineral sand form weird, weather-sculptured shapes; small freshwater streams run across the beach after rain, the endless surf rushes up to meet them and your bus can be shrouded in a cloud of spray.

Fraser Island is named after the captain of a ship, who, with his crew and pregnant English wife, was shipwrecked on the outer Great Barrier Reef on 21 May 1836. Though accounts of the event contradict each other, according to the most credible version the survivors, some mutinous, made a difficult boat journey – during which Mrs Fraser bore a stillborn child – to arrive at what was then called the Great Sand Island. All but the few who escaped were captured by Aborigines of various tribes, separated from one another, kept almost as slaves, and treated with terrible savagery. Captain Fraser, who was already ill, died on the

Above: lunch is served. **Left:** Wanggoolba Creek. **Right:** at Movieworld

island, apparently soon after being speared by Aborigines. Mrs Fraser and three others were finally rescued and returned to Moreton Bay on 22 August 1836, in shocking condition, three months after the shipwreck.

More beach driving takes you back to the ferry and Rainbow Beach, where you board the mainline coach. When you reach a charming, rustic haven called **Silky Oak Tea Gardens** on the road to Gympie, there will be a welcome stop for dinner. You'll be back in Brisbane by about 10.15pm or at the Gold Coast by 11.30pm.

13. A World of Worlds *(see pull-out map)*

At Sea World watch the Water Ski Spectacular and the Dolphin Cove Show; scare yourself silly at Dreamworld; see how films are made at Warner Brothers' Movie World; get drenched at Wet'n'Wild World.

These four 'worlds' offer various joint packages which provide cut-price options to include two or more in your 'world tour', so shop around. All four attractions are open 10am–5pm, with the exception of Wet'n Wild World, which changes its closing time according to the season.

Whatever your hobby or field of interest, the Gold Coast probably offers it in the form of a world, and at a special-promotion low admission charge. There's Bonsai World; Cable Ski World; Dreamworld; Frozen World; Sea World; Snooker World; Tropical Fruit World; Warner Brothers' Movie World; Wet'n' Wild World; the World of Bees to mention just a few – all dishing up folly, fun, fear, fact, fantasy and fast food. Each is good value if its product is to your personal taste. The quality of entertainment, service and food is kept high by constant inter-World competition for your money.

The Coast's most polished attractions are Sea World and three other big theme parks, all located 15 minutes' drive north of Surfers' Paradise on the Gold Coast Highway. At **Sea World** (tel: 5588 2222; www.seaworld.com.au) on the Southport Spit just north of Main Beach, you'll find smoothly-staged entertainment, all of it aquatic. Sea World began as a water-skiing display 30 years ago and has developed its performances in parallel with a privately funded programme of marine animal rescue and welfare that caters for injured

whales, dolphins, seals and sea lions. Broader marine-life research has helped Sea World create realistic marine environments as backdrops for its public spectacles. The **Water Ski Spectacular** (12.30pm and 4pm daily) features some of Australia's most talented skiers in a series of spectacularly choreographed and gracefully executed aqua-ballet routines. Human pyramids of up to 10 performers in three tiers water-ski behind a single boat, and individual skiers and groups perform amazing high-speed jumps and airborne spins and flips.

Another must-see here is the **Dolphin Cove Show** (10.45am and 3pm daily), in which perfectly trained underwater creatures join equally well-rehearsed humans in a series of dazzling displays in the world's largest naturalistic lagoon habitat. Dolphins leap from the water in perfect formation; in one act, Sea World's marine mammals and their trainers demonstrate their remarkable rapport as a trainer is launched skywards from the water by a dolphin, before the pair dive back into the sea in perfect formation. For an add-on price, you can snorkel with the dolphins.

Apprehension Addiction

If you've ever wondered how it feels to fall backwards off a 40-storey building, **Dreamworld** (tel: 5588 1111; www.dreamworld.com.au) does a couple of pretty good simulations on its **Tower of Terror**. In one, you're magnetically accelerated at high speed along a horizontal rail, before you ascend vertically, like a jet fighter zooming sharply upwards. You then decelerate with the suddeness of a ball that was thrown into the air, plummeting backwards towards your point of origin. The other simulation is comparable to a bungee jump. Winched slowly up the Tower of Terror, you're probably admiring the serene countryside when somebody (apparently) cuts the rope. Again, plummeting is a feature of the experience, but this time, just as you become certain that your last moments are at hand, your descent is arrested by a sophisticated magnetic deceleration system just above the ground.

If you're not an avid apprehension addict, Dreamworld offers a sliding scale of less alarming diversions, ranging from the Gravitron and the Wipeout to rides on roller coasters, whitewater raft, chairlifts, paddle steamers and trains. In addition to its thrills-and-spills activities, Dreamworld features an IMAX adventure theatre and also native (and some international) wildlife, including dingoes, kangaroos and koalas.

Right across the highway is **Warner Brothers' Movie World** (tel: 5573 8485; www.movieworld.com.au), another prime Gold Coast attraction. Movie World invites you to enjoy a well-presented, behind-the-scenes view of the special effects, and illusions involved in movie making. A fast-moving kaleidoscope of action, comedy, stunts, animatronics and fun enables the vis-

Top: a bumpy ride at Wet'n'Wild World

itor to all but join the actors in the excitement. As their movie theme parks proliferate in the US, Europe and Australia, the major Hollywood studios might wonder whether they are giving away too many secrets of the trade.

Wet Wet Wet

'Double the thrill and double the terror!' Though this is one of the pledges made by **Wet'n'Wild World** (tel: 5573 6233; www.wetnwild.com.au), you can enjoy plenty of wet'n'wildness while foregoing the terror altogether. The publicity tends to target youngsters, but there's usually a good representation of all age groups at Wet'n'Wild World. Two of the highlights are the **Giant Wave Pool** and a 15-minute tube ride along a slow-moving river from the simulated tropical island's **Calypso Beach.** You can spend a whole day just sunbathing and watching the activities, or you can get involved – and wet. Don't be deterred by cool weather – the water is heated all year round. If it's summer (when the attraction is open until 9pm) and you want to stay for a poolside barbecue, you might enjoy the drive-in movie screened at the pool.

14. Scenic Flights *(see pull-out map)*

On any good-weather day, you'll notice swarms of small aeroplanes and helicopters buzzing up and down the Coast. This is a relatively inexpensive way to gain a quick but comprehensive bird's-eye view of the Gold Coast, its magnificent hinterland and Mount Tamborine.

Getting in and out of a seaplane can involve wading or walking on wet sand, so it's a good idea to go barefoot or wear slip-on shoes.

The following central Gold Coast operators are recommended: **Air Waves** floatplane service (tel: 5564 0444), based at the end of the Marina Mirage jetty, takes four or five passengers and bumps across the wavelets to become airborne in seconds. The seaplane cruises across the Broadwater, along the beaches of the Strip, over the luxury canal developments or into a quiet bay on South Stradbroke Island, where you're likely to share the beach with wallabies accustomed to human contact. **Sea World Helicopters** (tel: 5588 2224), operating from the nearby Sea World theme park, offers similar sightseeing routes but in a vertical-takeoff mode in a six-passenger Longranger or four-passenger Jetranger. Five routes are available at a range of prices, and entrance to Sea World is not a precondition.

For the solo sightseer who is partial to an open-air aviation adventure, a latter-day Biggles, Geoff Stillman of **Tiger Moth Joy Rides** (tel: 5502 7855), takes passengers aboard his vintage biplane on flights from the Albatross Airfield on Abraham Road, Coomera, directly opposite Dreamworld. Your pilot will (on request) add an aerobatic dimension. Rest assured, he's very thorough when strapping you into the open cockpit.

Right: for the ultimate view of the Coast

Leisure Activities

SHOPPING

If you haven't already filled your shopping quota at the theme parks, hillside haunts and resort retailers, it may be time for a shopping spree. In both Brisbane and the Gold Coast, it's well worth checking out the big suburban supermarkets where parking is free and relatively easy, and where prices tend to be more attuned to local householders than to visitors who half-expect to be ripped off.

Brisbane's **Queen Street Mall,** the centre of the shopping scene, offers more than 500 speciality shops across two city blocks. The blocks are dominated by two large department stores, **Myers** and **David Jones**, which sell pretty much everything at quite competitive prices. In the pretty, heritage-listed **Brisbane Arcade** nearby, you'll find the work of Queensland's award-winning fashion designers. Logan Road, in Stone's Corner, is home to Brisbane's best factory seconds and second-hand designer clothing.

The Gold Coast features a number of ultra-large shopping complexes, primary among which is the **Surfers Paradise Centre** in Cavill Avenue, which employs meter maids in gold bikinis. The meter-maids initiative is a fairly successful example of a Chamber of Commerce attempt to put the Coast on the map. These ladies, something of a tourist attraction themselves, have saved many a shopper a parking fine. You'll have difficulty finding a parking space on the street at busy times, but there's ample underground parking at moderate charges.

Other major consumer centres of note are **The Oasis** shopping centre, Victoria Avenue; Broadbeach, adjoining Conrad Jupiter's Casino; **Pacific Fair**, Hooker Boulevard; and **Raptis Plaza**, The Esplanade (on the corner of Cavill Avenue). Of these, all but Raptis have supermarkets. A little further out – but only 10 minutes by free shuttlebus from the heart of Surfers – is the extensive new **Robina Town Centre** (off the Robina Parkway), which has more than 200 speciality shops, five major department stores, and six cinemas.

Australia-made

Some notable Australian manufacturers have outlets or stockists in key central shopping centres. Among them is **Akubra**, whose famous broad-brimmed felt hats are peculiar to Australia and hugely popular with overseas visitors. **R.M.Williams** (the Wintergarden, Queen Street Mall, stockists also on the Gold Coast), is known for the rugged-looking bushwear he has designed and sold to rural people for many years, and which has become an international style. Two popular products are his riding boots and Driza Bone raincoats. Artist **Ken Done** and his designer wife produce light and bright casual clothes, and **Brothers Neilsen** specialise in Australian-designed casual street-, beach- and surf-wear – and surfboards. From across the Tasman comes the tough and colourful **Canterbury** outdoor range and sportswear. Acklander and Emaroo produce a range of designer fashion knitwear made from 100 percent Australian wool. **Brian Rochford** is a popular Australian label for skimpy swimwear.

Australian-produced foodstuffs are becoming increasingly popular. These include

Left: taking a break at a Paddington café
Right: retro designs at a trendy outlet in Paddington

macadamias in various guises, tea and coffee from plantations in tropical north Queensland, koala-shaped pasta and, for adventurous carnivores, crocodile, shark or emu jerky.

Queensland's richly-coloured **boulder opals** are in ever-growing demand; as are the large and lustrous Australian **South Sea pearls**. Imaginative jewellers are now putting together creative works blending these with **Western Australian Argyll coloured diamonds**, ranging in hue from 'Champagne' and 'Cognac' to the rarer pinks. If you want to buy such lasting treasures, go to a reputable jeweller.

Although crocodiles are now a protected species, they are farmed commercially, and crocodile-skin bags, belts and shoes of several brands, although expensive, are a quality Australian product. So is sheepskin, in the form of rugs, jackets, slippers, seat covers and corny-looking stuffed lambs.

Aboriginal Art

Some Aboriginal art is 'fair dinkum' (Aussie for genuine), and some is mass-produced. For the former in Brisbane, try **Queensland Aboriginal Creations**, 199 Elizabeth Street, a respected showplace of Aboriginal and Torres Strait islander art and artefacts. The gallery also features exhibits by better-known artists, and the extensive stock of artefacts caters for all tastes and budgets. For the one-time buyer of memorabilia or indeed the serious collector, there is fine art on bark, which Aboriginal artists used before the advent of canvas and paper. Boomerangs, those famous examples of Aboriginal aerodynamics, are always popular; genuine returning models (as opposed to the strictly ornamental variety) come with instructions to help you throw them properly. You can practise this ancient art in any wide-open space: don't be tempted to have a fling in the hotel foyer, no matter how big it is. Authentic artefacts are on sale at the **Kalwun Development** souvenir shop, in the National Parks Information Centre at 1171 Gold Coast Highway, Tallebudgera.

It's said that the average Qantas aeroplane leaving Australia carries enough didgeridoos to start a corroboree (Aboriginal ceremonial dance). Be warned that didgeridoos don't fit in an overhead locker.

Markets

If you're in Brisbane on a Sunday morning, check out the **Eagle Street Pier Craft Market** (Sunday only) – the best of some dozen such markets in the city. It has the most imaginative assortment of handmade quality-crafted ceramics, woodwork, Aboriginal artefacts, leather goods, toys, confectionery and pretty baubles, to name just a few of its many consumer goods, all of which are sold under a canopy of colourful umbrellas.

The most reputable market on the Gold Coast is **Carrara Markets** (Sat–Sun 7am–4pm; tel: 5579 9388), Nerang-Broadbeach Road near Pacific Fair. Look out for locally-grown fresh fruit in season; there's a bus pickup from most hotels on the Strip.

Property

Seduced by the sun, sand and surf, more than a few visitors are attracted by the idea of owning a Gold Coast apartment and renting it out to holidaymakers between visits. Gold Coast Realtors, which runs several high-profile downtown offices, vigorously promote this proposition with elaborate displays and persuasive guarantees of returns in the order of eight percent, typically for two years. For new properties, foreign ownership is not a problem, but to buy old properties you need citizenship, residency, or ownership of an Australian company. Also, study the market – you wouldn't want your bubble to burst at the end of the two-year guarantee due to over-pricing of the property. There is currently no limit on the amount a non-Australian can invest, so if you have the means, you could find yourself buying a whole apartment block.

Left: boomerangs with authentic Aboriginal decoration

EATING OUT

If such figures mean anything, the Gold Coast has more than 5,000 restaurants, and Brisbane claims the highest number *per capita* of any city in Australia.

It would be easy to draw the unkind conclusion that Australia doesn't possess a culinary style of its own; but let's remember that the country has evolved through little more than 200 years of immigration from almost every country in the world, and that the resulting blend of cultures has enriched its dining tables with a huge diversity of cross-cultural concepts. Although British immigrants were in the majority, in the early days, Australia's menus were much enhanced by major waves of immigration from Italy, Greece, France, China, the Scandinavian countries and, more recently, southeast Asia. In deference to the generally warm subtropical climate, there is a definite avoidance of some of the heavy, stodgy menus of Europe. The country's status as a primary producer is reflected in both the freshness and the low cost of food: this applies to both supermarkets and restaurants. Beef (usually in the form of generous, juicy grilled steaks straight from Queensland's world-famous beef-producing regions) and seafood in all its indigenous variety, dominate the region's cuisine and in general offer the best value.

Strange though it might seem, in recent decades, yuppies have been responsible for improving the standard of local dining. Before their fall from grace in the last economic slump of the 20th century, yuppies, whose image tended to focus on public posturing rather than labours in the larder, made a significant contribution to the maturing of the country's restaurant cultures. Their fleeing wealth led to a rush of demand for quality dining, which in turn forced the somewhat lethargic restaurant industry to update its presentation and marketing. The new money heightened competition in quality, cost, and service. Those yuppies who survived the fall from economic grace are still enjoying that outcome: indeed, one of their chastened number may well be the person explaining the menu to you.

Wine

There's no need to bust the budget with imported wines when you're in Australia; the local wines are wonderful. They are rich in variety, diverse in flavour and style, and reasonably priced (although the mark-up at some restaurants is excessive). From the rich reds of Coonawarra to the delicate dry whites of the Clare Valley, Australia's wines are as disparate as its climate. The country's wine makers have long since

Top: Asian influences abound
Right: pizza and antipasto

completed their apprenticeship and are competing with considerable success on the international market. As a general guideline, if you're looking for oak-driven reds or whites, check out something from the Barossa Valley. If you want less oak, try the Hunter Valley, famous for wines made from pinot noir and chardonnay grapes. Whether or not you're celebrating a special occasion, treat yourself to a bottle of one of the country's finest *méthode champenoise* wines, which are surprisingly inexpensive.

Price ranges for a three-course meal for two without wine are as follows:

$ = AU$40 or less
$$ = AU$41-AU$60
$$$ = AU$61 or more

Brisbane

In Brisbane, there are several distinct dining neighbourhoods, each featuring variety and informality along with quality and reasonably modest prices. These precincts are all just a few minutes' cab drive from the central business district. They include **Paddington**, a trendy residential and pub area with lots of outdoor dining; **West End**, which is particularly diverse, though it has a pronounced Asian emphasis; **Milton**, which offers everything from deli-style cafés to silver-service dining, in a slightly more upmarket village atmosphere that complements a local cluster of galleries; **Brunswick Street**, which has a gallery-scullery ambience; and the **Chinatown Mall** in Fortitude Valley, which is Brisbane's home of multinational Asian cuisine, although also surrounded by a wide range of non-Asian cafés, coffee houses and restaurants. Two lunching and dining precincts on the city's outskirts are **South Bank**, just across the river by ferry or bridge, and the **Riverside Centre**, where several attractive restaurants overlooking the Brisbane River and the Storey Bridge offer a range of menus that call for hard decisions between rival temptations.

If you are spooked by licensed-restaurant prices, there are dozens of unlicensed BYO (bring your own wine) restaurants, many located strategically near liquor outlets. BYO eateries provide the wine-drinker's tools – corkscrews and glasses – and, dependent as they are on local custom, rarely disappoint.

Fine Dining

Michael's Riverside Restaurant
Riverside Centre
123 Eagle Street, Brisbane
Tel: 3832 5522
The offerings of Michael Platsis's restaurant include lovingly prepared Mediterranean dishes, Aussie steaks, and seafood,

along with a range of native poultry dishes. For a fine potpourri of Australian 'bush tucker', the 'hunter's game grill' – a feast of kangaroo, pigeon and water-buffalo tenderloin, green trimmings and a truffle honey glaze – is recommended. If you tackle this dish, you'll be glad that you had a light breakfast. Open 11.30am till late. *$$$*

Pier Nine Seafood Restaurant
Eagle Street Pier by the river
Tel: 3229 2194
This restaurant presents such an array of fresh Queensland seafoods that its menu is a geography refresher course: sand crabs from the shallow sandy bays, prawns (shrimps) from the Gulf of Carpentaria, delicious coral trout from the Great Barrier Reef's blue expanses, and tropical estuary barramundi. It serves up to eight different varieties of oysters in three different ways, and offers relaxing river views. There's no better place to enjoy the huge estuary barramundi, one of northern Australia's most famous fish. Popular with fishermen who appreciate cunning and tenacity in a quarry, it is highly prized by the gourmet for its tenderness and flavour. Open 11.30am–10pm for à la carte. *$$$*

China House Seafood Restaurant
12 Duncan Street in 'The Valley'
Tel: 3216 0570
If you're feeling adventurous, go for the Singapore chilli mud crab. It's unclear whether it's the chilli or the mud crab that originates in Singapore, but the world mud crab capital, the Gladstone/Rockhampton district, is a few hundred miles north of Brisbane. Open daily 10am–3pm, 5–11pm. *$$*

Mount Coot-tha Summit Restaurant
Sir Samuel Griffith Drive, Brisbane
Tel: 3369 9922
Elevated vista of the city lights. From the char-grill, try the eye fillet steak with a Gulf prawn-tails seafood accompaniment. Mon–Sat 11.30am–late, Sun 8am–late. *$$$*

Thai Ayuthaya Restaurant
Chermside Place
725 Gympie Road
Chermside
Tel: 3350 2828

Authentic Thai food always served with a warm smile. Open for dinner daily 5.30–10.30pm. *$$*

Nataraja Indian Restaurant
152 Musgrave Road
Red Hill
Tel: 3369 2455
Wednesday night is the best time to visit Nataraja because that's when the smorgasbord features the restaurant's butter-chicken speciality. Open 11.30am–2pm, 5.30pm till late, closed Mon. *$$*

Oxley's on the River
330 Coronation Drive
Tel: 3368 1866
This charming restaurant juts out over the water. A house speciality is barbecued Moreton Bay bugs. Don't be put off by the dish's name: its devotees claim this lobster-like creature is the genuine king of the crustaceans. Open daily 11.30am–2.30pm, 5.30–10pm. *$$$*

Ecco
100 Boundary Street, City
Tel: 3831 8344
A prize-winning bistro. Try steamed mussels with saffron chilli and ginger, followed by a juicy Australian steak or Atlantic salmon. Open Tues–Fri from noon for lunch, Tues–Sat from 6pm for dinner. *$$$*

Above left: local wines. **Left:** sundae treats
Above right: high dining at Mount Coot-tha Summit Restaurant

Il Centro Restaurant and Bar
Eagle Street Pier
Tel: 3221 6090
Wonderful pasta (try the delicious sand crab lasagne), steak and seafood. Booking essential. Open daily noon–3pm for lunch and 6–10pm for dinner. *$$$*

Gambaro
33 Caxton Street
Petrie Terrace
Tel: 3369 9500
Sample one of the seafood platters, which are a real gastronomic delight. Open weekdays for lunch noon–2pm and Mon–Sat from 6pm till late. The oyster bar opposite is open Sun–Thur for lunch and Sun–Fri nights for dinner. *$$$*

Pine & Bamboo Restaurant
Shop 7
968 Wynnum Road
Cannon Hill
Tel: 3399 9462
This is an excellent and inexpensive Chinese restaurant that is extremely popular with the local population, for good reason. The proprietor Bill Wong is a spontaneous, helpful and entertaining host. Open daily 11.30am–3pm for lunch, 6pm till late for dinner. *$$*

Lunches, Brunches, & Munches

Customs House Brasserie
399 Queen Street
Tel: 3365 8921
If you're out for a Sunday brunch after a shopping session at the Eagle Street Markets (*see Shopping, page 72*), you should sample the fresh oysters *au natural* with a Chardonnay vinegar and eschalot dressing, fresh coriander and lime wedges. Open daily from 10am. *$$*

Breakfast Creek Hotel
2 Kingsford Smith Drive
Breakfast Creek
Tel: 3257 1999
The Brekkie's rump, fillet, sirloin and T-bone steaks are virtually the size of a dinner plate, and are consistently thick, juicy, and flavoursome. Choose your own steak at the barbecue in the Staghorn Beer garden and, while you're waiting, enjoy a beer 'off the wood' (drawn from a wooden keg on the bar). This is quite a rare opportunity to enjoy a draught beer – Australians in general seem to prefer more high-tech ways of storing lager. For those who find the local parlance a little confusing: 'Just knock the horns off it and walk it past the grill, mate', means: 'a large steak, very rare, please'. *$*

Above: watch the chef at work at The Fireplace, Sanctuary Cove

Gold Coast

Here it's generally a good idea to avoid most of the more expensive hotel dining establishments, the slick but sloppy inner-Coast diners (where the routine is strictly order, eat and leave) and the franchises. Rather, seek out the smaller, owner-operated dining venues. There are loads of these along the Coast outside the most concentrated shopping areas, along the highway to the south and in the Main Beach neighbourhood.

The Broadbeach Tavern
Old Burleigh Road
corner of Charles Avenue
Broadbeach
Tel: 5538 4111
At this restaurant you'll find quality lunches and dinners from an extensive, and surprisingly inexpensive, menu. A variety of guest bands enliven the atmosphere with the sound of music, and assorted jokers, clowns and stand-up merchants entertain diners on Wednesday's comedy night. Lunch 12noon–2pm; dinner 6–8pm Mon–Sat. *$*

Volare Restaurant
2729 Gold Coast Highway
Broadbeach
Tel: 5592 2622
Proprietor Nino Miano and his team treat customers like family. The whole atmosphere – sights, sounds, aromas and frescoes – is redolent of old Italy. Try the *zuppa di pesce* dish (mixed seafood drenched in a spicy tomato sauce). Open 10.30am–2.30pm and 6pm till late. *$$$*

Top: grilled to perfection
Right: a fruit shake and slice

The Rez Two Fifty Two Restaurant
Courtyard Surfers Paradise Resort
Corner of the Gold Coast Highway and Hanlam Street
Tel: 5579 3499
For a special but quite expensive night out, this restaurant offers the best in contemporary Australian cuisine. Fresh local-seafood dishes and tropical fruits are daily features. Open 5.30–about 9pm. *$$$*

The Fireplace
The Hyatt Regency
Sanctuary Cove
Tel: 5530 1234
If you're not deterred by the expense, this is a truly wonderful gastronomic experience. The chefs prepare your meal in the restaurant itself, where you can watch them deploying their considerable talents. The ambience is opulent and supremely comfortable, and the silver service is impeccable. The seafood grills, or perhaps a grain-fed yearling sirloin, are recommended. Open daily 6–10pm. *$$$*

Horizons Restaurant
The Sheraton Mirage
Main Beach
Tel: 5591 1488
One of the Coast's finest restaurants. Is the absence of external views deliberate? Perhaps the owners don't want you to be distracted from appreciating your meal. *$$$*

NIGHTLIFE

In all Australian nightclubs, bars and casinos, entry is restricted to over-18s; the young and young-looking may have to show ID. Late-night entertainment ranges from international stars in world-class venues to nude table-top dancing in dimly-lit dives.

Performing Arts

Brisbane has a flourishing performing arts scene. The **Queensland Performing Arts Complex** (Info line: 3846 4444) at the Queensland Cultural Centre in the South Bank Precinct is the major hub for the city's cultural entertainment. Its rich programme includes theatre, musicals, opera, ballet and concerts. Cinemas are plentiful, comfortable and reasonably priced. Listings are printed in the daily *Courier Mail*.

The Schonell Theatre
St Lucia University campus
Brisbane
Tel: 3377 2229
This theatre screens a wide variety of films, commercial and arty, and also hosts live performances. Check ads in the *Courier Mail* on Thursdays and Saturdays. Special rates for local and international students.

La Boite Repertory Theatre
Corner Hale and Sexton Streets
Brisbane City 4000
Tel: 3010 2600
A theatre in the round specialising in sharp contemporary Australian theatre. Five or six plays are staged each year.

Top: performance at La Boite
Right: a favourite Brisbane venue

The Gold Coast Art Centre
135 Bundall Road, Bundall
Tel: 5588 4000
The Coast's nocturnal culture revolves around this centre. Besides its high-quality art gallery, it features movies and theatre, and there's something happening seven days a week. Live performances tend to be a blend of Australian and international, old and new, and Friday night is comedy night. There's also a cabaret restaurant.

Nightclub, Disco and Bar Entertainment

The heart of Brisbane's nightlife is Fortitude Valley, which everybody calls 'The Valley'. For an up-to-date 'gig guide', consult *Pulse*, the Brisbane *Courier Mail*'s Friday insert. Also *Time Off*, a free weekly handout, is available at most music stores, pubs and clubs. Few such venues apply cover charges, and most will let you in if you're wearing shoes.

Around the Caxton Street/Petrie Terrace intersection precinct a number of complementary venues overlap one another. Leading the pack are: **The Cassablanca** brasserie (tel: 3369 6969), bar, café and a really steamy cellar club; the **Hotel LA** (tel: 3368 2560) – a lively scene with lots of sounds, best for under 35s; and **Gambaro's Restaurant** (33 Caxton Street, Petrie Terrace; tel: 3369 9500), Brisbane's top seafood restaurant.

Ric's Cafe-Bar
321 Brunswick Street
Tel: 3854 1772
This classic venue supports and promotes young artists and local music – jazz, funk, electronica – and is open until around 5am. At closing time, lots of patrons go straight next door to Fat Boys (24 hours, Thurs–Sat) for a cheap breakfast.

P J O'Brien's Irish Pub
127 Charlotte Street
Tel: 3210 6822
A good, lively night scene. The entertainment is provided by the customers themselves. Adjoins the **Adrenalin Sports Bar**.

The Press Club
Empire Hotel
339 Brunswick Street
Fortitude Valley
Tel: 3852 1216
Offers a plush lounge bar with live bands Wed and Sun and a DJ other nights, and a vodka bar specialising in jazz, blues, funk. Open till 5am every night except Sun (3am).

The Zoo
711 Ann Street
Tel: 3854 1381
Very big on live bands, but also features DJs to broaden the musical mix. At night, drinks are sold but not food. Open Tue–Sun.

The Story Bridge Hotel
196 Main Street
Kangaroo Point
Brisbane
Tel: 3391 2266
The hotel is situated under the famous bridge, and its Bomb Shelter Bar, built by the US forces in 1942, is still a top spot to get bombed. Live blues bands, Thurs–Sat.

Dracula's
1 Hooker Boulevard
Broadbeach Waters
Tel: 5575 1000
Australia's longest-established dinner theatre featuring magic, puppetry, musical productions and great comedy. Three-course dinner with live cabaret, Tues–Sat.

The Base Supper Club
corner of Elizabeth Avenue and Gold Coast Highway
Tel: 5592 5527
This cabaret restaurant wows its clientèle with live entertainment, much of it a musical mystery tour of pop, rock and soul, but also featuring comedy acts. If you're hungry, this is the place for a slap-up dinner. Open Wed–Sat, booking essential.

Right: place your bets

Island Queen Showboat Cruises
Tel: 5557 8800
A floating venue, with cheap coach pickup, for a fine seafood buffet dinner. Entertainment includes Polynesian dancers.

Big Clubs and Casinos

The big clubs on the border are subsidised by gaming machines that keep the excellent entertainment free and the meals inexpensive. Two of the most popular are **Seagulls** (Gollan Drive, Tweed Heads; tel: 5536 3433) and the **Twin Towns Services Club** (Pacific Highway, Tweed Heads; tel: 5536 2277). You must sign in at reception and show proof that you're a *bona fide* visitor.

When in Brisbane, the place to flirt with fortune is the **Treasury Casino** (tel: 3306 8888). Located at the top end of Queen Street in the restored Treasury Building (one of Brisbane's finest landmarks), the casino is open 24 hours every day. There's free live entertainment nightly and, as well as the 100-odd gaming tables, there are more than 1,100 gaming machines. There are also five restaurants, to suit every taste, and seven bars.

A popular gambling haunt among Gold Coast visitors is **Conrad Jupiters** (Gold Coast Highway, Broadbeach; tel: 5592 1133; www.conrad.com.au), open 24 hours. This casino and entertainment resort has two floors of gaming tables, a nightclub, themed restaurants and bars, plus world-class live shows.

Natural Nightlife

The Glow-worm tour from the Gold Coast. (Aries Tours; tel: 5594 9933; www.aries-tours.com) is a bit of far-out fun for the nature lover. After a three-course dinner, head into the hills for a nocturnal nature walk, especially entertaining when the frogs are in full chorus. The glow-worms glowing at the Natural Bridge are a spectacular sight.

CALENDAR OF EVENTS

The following events only scratch the surface of what's happening. Call the tourism authorities (*see page 91*) for further information about current events.

Brisbane

January/February

26 January: Australia Day entertainment at South Bank as part of the national holiday celebrating the country's independence. Tel: 3867 2051.

Early February–Early November: Queensland Youth Symphony Concert Series; there is usually a series of six concerts. Tel: 3257 1191.

Mid-February: Chinese New Year/Spring Festival. Festivities take place in Chinatown Mall. Tel: 3252 5999.

Top: celebrations in Chinatown
Above: competing in the Gold Coast Indy

March/April

17 March: St Patrick's Day celebrations – not exclusive to those with Irish ancestry – swathe Queen Street Mall in a mass of green. Tel: 3229 7833.

Early April: Brisbane to Gladstone Yacht Race. Tel: 3269 4588.

April–November: Musica Viva Australia – an international series of concerts, Queensland Conservatorium. Tel: 3875 6229.

Mid-April–end June: Queensland Winer Racing Carnival. Details from the Brisbane Turf Club. Tel: 3268 6800.

25 April: Anzac Day – commemorative dawn services are held at Returned Servicemen's League clubs across the country.

May/June

5–8 May: Commemoration of the Battle of the Coral Sea. Tel: 5535 0506.

Late May: Brisbane River Run and Walk. Tel: 3349 1459.

1 June–1 November: Whale watching. Tel: 3409 9336.

6 June: Queensland Day celebrations staged by members of Queensland Performing Arts. Tel: 3377 5000.

July/August

Mid- to late July: Queensland Biennial Festival of Music; various venues. Tel: 3840 7958. Alternates with Brisbane Festival.

Early August: Royal Easter Show, RNA Showgrounds ('The Ekka'), Brisbane – 10 days. Tel: 3852 1831.

September/October

The River Festival – various river locations; food/entertainment, aquatic events, fireworks, etc. Tel: 3403 8888.
Brisbane Festival, various locations, staged by Queensland Performing Arts every other year. Alternates with the Queensland Biennial Festival of Music. Tel: 3840 7444.
Mid-October–mid-March: Sheffield Shield cricket at the Woolloongabba cricket ground. Tel: 3292 3100.

November/December

Christmas Lantern Festival, Riverside. Tel: 3867 2051.

Gold Coast

All Year

There's almost always a surf lifesaving event during the weekend. Tel: 3846 8000.

January/February

January: Conrad Jupiters Magic Millions horse racing carnival. Tel: 5538 1599.
January: Kellogs Nutrigrain iron man series, Surfers' Paradise beach.
Late February: Australian Ladies' Masters golf tournament, Royal Pines Resort. Tel: 5597 1111.

March/April/May

Late March: Australian Surf Lifesaving Championships – contests take place over five days. Tel: 9130 7370.
April–weekend before Easter: Canungra Camp Draft – stockmen pit their skills against one another on horseback.
Late May: Celicia Annual Billfish Tournament, Sanctuary Cove. Tel: 5553 8400.

June/July

June: Wintersun Festival, Coolangatta; a ten-day festival with a rock'n'roll nostalgia theme. Tel: 5536 9509.
7 June–7 July: International games – the largest gridiron tournament outside the US. Tel: 5527 6799.
4 July: American Independence Day and street parade – American expats, tourists and anyone who wants to celebrate gather at the Hard Rock Café, Cavill Avenue, corner of Gold Coast Highway. Tel: 5539 9377.
Early July: Tweed Bowls Open – mixed singles. World's richest outdoor bowls tournament. Tel: 5536 3800.
Mid-July: Gold Coast Marathon, Broadwater to Southport. Tel: 5564 8733.

August/September

Late August: Gold Coast Show, Parklands Showground. Tel: 5591 3422.

October/November/December

Early October: Springtime on the Mountain garden and flower festival – displays of native and exotic flowers at Mount Tambourine showgrounds. Tel: 5545 1271.
Mid-October: Gold Coast Indy 300, Surfers' Paradise – four days of in-city motor racing. Tel: 5588 6800.
Early November: Bird Week, O'Reilly's Rainforest Guest House. Australia's most popular bird-watching week. Tel: 5544 0644.
Late November: Schoolies' Week. The Gold Coast is invaded by young Australians who have just completed their secondary education. If you are looking for rest and relaxation on the Coast, you may want to avoid this period.
27 December–1 January: Themed arts and culture-based folk festival with workshops, craft stalls, and a dramatic fire ceremony on 1 January. Tel: 5496 1066.
Late December: A mounting crescendo of frenzied festivity.

Above: aquatic events take place throughout the year

CityCat

Practical Information

GETTING THERE

By Air

Many international airlines provide regular links between Brisbane and Europe, New Zealand, Japan, the US and Asian and Pacific nations. Frequent Qantas and Virgin Blue domestic services fly from Brisbane and Coolangatta (the Gold Coast's domestic airport) to Sydney, Melbourne, Canberra and other state capitals, and to all of Queensland regional centres north to Cairns. Overseas travellers are offered domestic fares free of goods and services tax on production of an international ticket and a passport.

By international standards, Australian domestic aircraft offer comfortable seating and good service. Published fares are high, but a growing and competitive jumble of off-peak deals are offered, especially advance-purchase returns with even lower fares if you're staying over on a Saturday night. These might be better deals than any international discount you may qualify for.

Brisbane Airport's adjacent international and domestic terminals are connected by shuttle bus. Few hotels provide regular courtesy coach transfers, but a few will do so on request. Cabs to the city are expensive. However, a combination of comfortable, regular Airport Commuter coaches and a fast shuttle train takes you to and from the central city terminal at Roma Street with shuttles from there to many of the downtown hotels. "Transinfo" (tel: 131230) can provide all the travel information you need.

Earliest and latest rail transfers available are weekdays 5.30am/8.30pm, Sat 5.30am/8.25pm, Sun 6.10am/8.25pm. The Gold Coast is not an international gateway. Arrivals from abroad are normally transferred and have to travel from Brisbane to the Coast by coach and rail (again, enquire from Transinfo.) Air services between Brisbane and the Coast are few and far between; coach or train is far quicker.

Left: Citycat ferry
Right: watch out for echidnas on the road

By Rail

Brisbane's main rail terminal is the Transit Centre in Roma Street, which is a short taxi ride from most Brisbane hotels. Fast trains travel to Robina on the Gold Coast, from 4am to 11pm, at half-hour intervals for most of the day, dwindling to one an hour during less busy times. (Call Transinfo on 131230 for timetable information.) Connections to Surfers' Paradise, Southport and other Coast destinations are provided by Surfside Buslines.

By Road

The road between Brisbane and the Gold Coast is excellent. The main highway between Sydney and Brisbane is variable but adequate, the journey normally taking about 12 hours, not including stops. Driving around Brisbane and the Gold Coast is relatively easy, although some Brisbane streets can become congested; and inner-city one-way streets in both centres can be confusing.

TRAVEL ESSENTIALS

When to Visit

Any time is a good time. The weather is mild in winter, spring and autumn, and you can escape the summer heat and humidity (December to March) by going up into the hills, onto the beach or staying by the pool (*see Weather, overleaf*).

Visas and Passports

Your passport must be valid for at least six months from your date of arrival. All non-Australian citizens need a valid visa to enter Australia, with the exception of New Zealand citizens travelling on New Zealand passports, who are issued with a visa on arrival in Australia. Visas are available from Australian visa offices such as Australian embassies, high commissions and consulates; and from travel agents and airlines in some countries.

Airlines may turn away travellers who don't have valid visas and passports; potential visitors should obtain their visas before purchasing airline tickets or entering into any other financial commitments dependent upon entry to Australia. Tourists are not allowed to work during their visit. Tourist visas are normally valid for 12 months, during which time you may make as many visits as you like for up to three months at a time.

Vaccinations

No vaccinations are necessary for entry into Australia unless you have visited an area (including parts of South America and Africa) infected by yellow fever, cholera or typhoid in the previous 14 days .

Customs

Non-dutiable allowances are 250g (8oz) of tobacco goods (approximately a carton of cigarettes) and 1125ml (a quart) of beer, wine or spirits, and other dutiable goods to the total value of £200, plus personal clothing, footwear and toiletries. Up to £100-worth of dutiable goods, not including alcohol or tobacco, are allowed in the baggage of children under 18.

Strict quarantine regulations forbid the importation of foods, plants, animals and their by-products. Animal disease is a major concern in the island continent, and the quarantine period for cats and dogs (including seeing-eye dogs) is six months, with the owner responsible for the payment of all costs. Heavy jail penalties apply to the smuggling of drugs of any kind. Visitors are allowed to carry up to four weeks' supply of prescribed medications, but for larger supplies you should carry a doctor's certificate for Customs purposes.

Weather

Brisbane enjoys an average of eight hours of sunshine for every day of the year, compared with Sydney's seven and Melbourne's five. Brisbane's annual rainfall is 1,146mm (45in). The Gold Coast doesn't keep sunshine records, but they are similar to Brisbane, while its rainfall is slightly higher at 1,455mm (57in) annually. The climate is subtropical, with Brisbane's average maximum/minimum temperatures running from 28°/20°C (84°/69°F) in January (summer) to July's (winter) 20°C/9°C (68°/49°F). These figures add up to good, sunny, warm weather for an unusually high number of days in the year.

Clothing

In the subtropical climate, dress is informal and casual. Don't bring an umbrella because you may not need it, and they're cheap in the supermarkets. Lightweight clothing is suitable year-round, but bring something warm in case the temperature at night drops, especially in the autumn and winter. Some hotels, restaurants and clubs require a jacket and tie in the evening. If susceptible to sunstroke and sunburn, you should wear a broad-brimmed hat, and a shirt with collar and sleeves to protect your neck and arms. Bring swimwear and sunglasses for the beach.

Right: trying it on for size

Electricity
Electrical power is 240/250v AC, 50Hz Universal. Most hotels also have outlets for 110v (shavers only). Australian power outlets are an unusual three-pin configuration, but adaptors are readily available in shops and hotels.

Time differences
Queensland operates on Australian Eastern Standard Time (Greenwich Mean Time minus 10 hours). Daylight saving is not observed in Queensland, but does apply, from different dates, in the other states across three time zones, giving, at worst, up to six differing times across the country.

GETTING ACQUAINTED

Geography
The region covered in this book is in the extreme southeast corner of Queensland. Almost two-thirds of the state's 3.5 million population live within 100km (60 miles) of Brisbane, occupying less than one percent of the state. The populated coastal strip north to Port Douglas accounts for the majority of the remaining population. The Great Dividing Range runs close to the Eastern coastline, all the way to Cape York, 800km (500 miles) north of Port Douglas. Vast, sparsely populated tracts of tropical rainforest, savanna, semi-arid plains and desert make up the rest of Queensland, which has a total area of about the combined size of France, Germany, Italy and Spain. It is all interesting country.

Government and Economy
Voting in federal and state elections is compulsory for all Australians aged over 18. Unlike most state parliaments, Queensland's does not have an upper and a lower house, which makes for a very straightforward way of doing things. The state's conservative and labour-oriented parties have always tended to be a little more polarised than their counterparts in other states, which brings extra spice, if not spite, to parliamentary debates. Many would argue that Queensland's progress has been enviably steady despite some of the parliament's high-profile antics. Politics becomes even more colourful at the third level – that of local government – with Brisbane and the Gold Coast often leading the field in media spectacle.

Queensland's economy is very dependent on the agriculture, natural-resource and tourism industries. The state's affluence is supported by – and is a reflection of – unusually high levels of both industrial and residential development.

MONEY MATTERS

Currency
Australia's currency consists of five-, 10-, 20-, 50- and 100-dollar notes, each of which has a distinctly different colour. The notes' unusual design and texture make them very difficult to forge. Whereas the five-, 10-, 20- and 50-cent coins are made from silver-coloured alloy, the one- and two-dollar coins

Above: watersports are an enduring attraction of the region

are gold-coloured. Watch out for the one-dollar coin which, confusingly, is larger than its two-dollar brother. Shopkeepers round up change to the nearest five cents.

Banks, cash machines, transfers and foreign exchange

Banks are open daily from 9.30am to 4pm except Friday, when they close at 5pm. Most have automatic teller machines. The banks and major retail outlets will change travellers' cheques and many hotels will change foreign currency at a slight premium. All international airports, banks and currency exchanges will change most common overseas currencies. If you're changing large amounts, banks usually give the best rates.

Credit Cards

Most establishments display a list of the credit cards they will accept, usually including Mastercard, Visa, Amex, Diners and JCB.

Within Australia, 24-hour credit card help numbers are:

- Visa/MasterCard: 1800 033103
- Amex: 1800 230100
- Diners: 1300 360060
- JCB: (Mon–Fri 9am–5pm) 02 9247 6399 (Japanese)

Tipping

Tipping is not customary. Tips aren't expected by taxi drivers, restaurant staff or hairdressers; on the other hand it's not unusual to reward good service, usually with a gratuity of up to 10 percent of the bill. Hotel staff do not solicit or expect tips, but won't be offended if you give one.

Departure Tax

The airlines grudgingly collect government airport tax by simply adding it to the cost of your ticket, so if you have a prepaid return ticket, you've already paid it.

GETTING AROUND

Hire Cars

Driving is relatively easy because the main thoroughfares are wide and well-signposted. You drive on the left side of the road. Although signposting is mostly good, you should arm yourself with road maps, which most rental companies provide. The large rental companies offer overseas visitors considerable discounts on pre-booked hire-cars.

Taxis

Taxis showing a light can be flagged down from the kerb. Rates per km are around $1 (50p). A small phone booking fee is charged, and most cabs take credit cards. Taxis normally carry only four passengers, but maxi-cabs, which take six to 10 passengers, are available on request at 1½ times normal rates. Smoking is banned in all cabs, and the passenger may be fined if not wearing a seatbelt. Phone numbers:
Brisbane Black & White Cabs: 131008;
Brisbane Yellow Cabs: 131924;
Gold Coast Regent Taxis: 131008;
Tweed Heads Coolangatta Taxis: 5536 1144.

HOURS & HOLIDAYS

Business Hours

Retailers enjoy flexible trading hours, especially in tourist shopping precincts. Outside the core business hours (9am–5.30pm Mon–Thurs, closing 9pm Fri in the cities; 9am–1pm Sat), traders tend to follow the demand, and hours vary widely.

Public Holidays

Banks, post offices, government and private offices close on the following holidays:

New Year's Day (1 Jan)
Australia Day (26 Jan)
Anzac Day (25 April)
Good Friday (date variable)

Above: take a taxi

Queen's Birthday (2nd Monday in June)
Labour Day (First Monday in May)
Christmas Day (25 Dec)
Boxing Day (26 Dec)

Market Days

Brisbane

Lantern Market: Fri 5pm-10pm, South Bank Parkland.
Village Markets: Sat 9am–3pm, Brunswick Street Mall, Chinatown.
Craft Village Variety Market: Sat 11am–5pm, South Bank Parkland.
Eagle Street Pier & Riverside Market: Sun 8am–4pm, Eagle Street, City.
Variety Market: Sun 9am–5pm, South Bank Parkland.

Gold Coast

Beach Front Market: Friday 5.30–10pm, Esplanade Boardwalk, Surfers' Paradise.
Carrara Market: Sat–Sun 6.30am–3.30pm, Nerang-Broadbeach Road near Pacific Fair.

ACCOMMODATION

The region has a huge number and range of accommodation facilities, and you are unlikely to have difficulty finding a place to stay unless there's a major event in progress. Information centres, including the airport accommodation desks, provide free guides; the best bet to combine your preferred style and location of accommodation is to read a guide in conjunction with a map.

If you're in doubt, don't be afraid to ask for permission to inspect a room before you make your decision. The best accommodation information is undoubtedly in *Jason's Guide*, a free publication that covers the whole of Queensland. In Brisbane, you can also obtain accommodation information at the information centres at the airport, King George Square or the Transit Centre in Roma Street. Alternatively, phone Brisbane Tourism on 3221 8411.

On the Gold Coast, where there are some 55,000 commercial bed spaces to choose from, *Jason's Guide* is the number-one reference. Again, you can also enquire at any information centre, or phone the Gold Coast Tourism Bureau (tel: 5592 2699).

Above: chilling out

Hotels

When booking your hotel accommodation, there's some latitude for striking a deal for longer stays, weekend rates, standby rates and so on. It is always worth asking about 'specials'. Many hotels have rooms for non-smokers; request these when booking.

The price ranges quoted in the following listings for a single or double room do not include luxury suites, which are available at most of the up-market hotels. The ranges given overlap because of the variety of room prices at some hotels.

Try these websites for hotel information:
www.holidaycity. com/brisbane-hotels
www.goldcoastburleightourism.com.au

Expensive: $200 upwards

Conrad International
130 William Street, Brisbane 4000
Tel: 1800 506889 (reservations)
House: 3306 8888
Fax: 3306 8880
www.conrad.com.au
Award-winning hotel located in the beautiful former Land Administration building that now houses the Treasury Casino complex. The hotel is ideally situated right in the heart of Brisbane – most of the city's big department stores are only a block or two away – and has views of the river across the street. All facilities.

Conrad International
Broadbeach Island, Broadbeach
Gold Coast, Queensland 4218
Tel: 1800 074344 (reservations)
House: 5592 1133
Fax: 5592 8219
www.conrad.com.au
Luxury suites also available. Houses Conrad Jupiter's casino. World-class in-house entertainment nightly, and a nifty little monorail to the nearby Oasis shopping complex.

Dockside Apartment Hotel
44 Ferry Street, Kangaroo Point
Brisbane 4169
Tel: 1800 775005 (reservations)
House: 3891 6644
Fax: 3891 6900
www.seqrents.com/au/dockside
Each spacious apartment has a fully-equipped kitchen and a balcony with a sweeping view. It's across the river from the city centre, but there's a ferry at the bottom of the garden. Can be very economical for a group or family.

Courtyard Surfers Paradise Resort
Corner Gold Coast Highway & Hanlan Street, Surfers Paradise, Gold Coast
Queensland 4217
Tel: 1800 074317 (reservations)
House: 5579 3499
Fax: 5592 0026
www.courtyard.com
High-quality accommodation, very central to everything in Surfers Paradise, with all facilities. For a great view of the surf, ask for a room from the 20th floor upwards.

Stamford Plaza Hotel
Corner Margaret & Edward Streets
Brisbane
Tel: 1800 773700 (reservations)
House: 3221 1999
Fax: 3221 6895
www.stamford.com.au
The Stamford Plaza is a classy heritage hotel with good restaurants; all of its rooms have river views, and it is close to the city's main attractions.

Palazzo Versace
Sea World Drive, Main Beach
Tel: 1800 098000
Fax: 5509 8888
www.palazzoversace.com
The ultimate in Renaissance splendour and luxury is expressed in the 205 rooms, the first venture into hotels by the Italian designer. The hotel has already set a new record (of $3,900 a night for its top suite).

Mid-range: $140–$250

Carlton Crest Hotel
Corner of Ann and Roma Streets
Brisbane 4000
Tel: 1800 777123 (reservations)
House: 3229 9111
Fax: 3229 9618
www.carltonhotels.com.au
Right opposite King George Square, close to

Above: the Regatta Hotel, an old-style hotel cum pub

the river and central shopping district, this recently modernised hotel is good value.

Country Comfort Lennons Hotel
66 Queen Street, City, Brisbane 4000
Tel: 3222 3222
Fax: 3221 9389
www.constellationhotels.com.au
A 20-storey tower in the city's heart, opposite Myers on the Mall. 152 units plus suites, non-smoking floors. Good value.

Chifley on George Hotel
103 George Street, Brisbane 4000
Tel: 1800 065064 (reservations)
House: 3221 6044
Fax: 3221 7474
www.constellationhotels.com.au
Five minutes' walk to city, casino or government district. Recently refurbished, heated outdoor pool and gymnasium. The popular spa rooms overlook the river and South Bank.

Goodearth Hotel
345 Wickham Terrace, Brisbane 4000
Tel: 1800 777789 (reservations)
House: 3831 6177
Fax: 3832 5919
www.goodearth.com.au
Prices include breakfast. There are 167 units in this hotel, which is situated close to Queen Street Mall and Central Station. It features excellent views of the city.

Calypso Plaza
87–105 Griffith Street, Coolangatta Queensland 4225
Tel: 1800 062189 (reservations)
House: 5599 0000
Fax: 5599 0099
www.theoaksrhm.com.au
This attractive, low-rise resort hotel is well away from the high-rise strip, near the surf beach, with a tropical swimming lagoon and water slide. The Calypso regularly offers specials, so be sure to ask when you book.

Modest: nothing over $150

(Except in some cases a suite or two)

Hotel Grand Chancellor
Corner Wickham Terrace and Leichhardt Street
Tel: 3913 6030
Fax: 3947 50180
On the crest of Spring Hill, the highest point in the city. Just minutes away from Southbank or the Treasury Casino. Majestic river, city and mountain views from every room.

Northgate Airport Motel
186 Toombul Road, Northgate Brisbane 4013
Tel: 3256 7222
Fax: 3256 7277
The closest motel to the airport, it has 25 beautifully appointed suites. Recommended if you're hiring a car because you're far from city traffic and parking problems.

Airport International Motels
528 Kingsford Smith Drive, Hamilton Brisbane 4007
Tel: 3268 6388
Fax: 3268 7395
www.airportmotel.com.au
Eight serviced self-contained apartments and 36 suites near the international and domestic air terminals. A short walk to the village-style shopping centre at Hamilton.

Hill Haven Holiday Apartments
2 Goodwin Terrace, Burleigh Head Gold Coast, Queensland 4220
Tel: 5535 1055
Fax: 5535 1870
Self-contained two- and three-bedroom holiday apartments, adjoining Burleigh Head National Park. All rooms have ocean views.

Pelican Cove on the Broadway
Corner Back and Burrows Streets, Surfers Paradise, Gold Coast, Queensland 4217
Tel: 5537 7001
Fax: 5537 7438
www.pelicancove.com.au
Two- and three-bedroom self-contained units right on the waterfront, 10 minutes from Wet'n'Wild World, Dream World, and (by water taxi) Sea World.

All Seasons' Mermaid Waters Hotel
Corner Markeri and Sunshine Boulevard Mermaid Waters
Tel: 1800 674087 (reservations)
House: 5572 2500
Fax: 5572 9787

www.asia-hotels.com/hotelinfo/All_Seasons
More than 100 rooms, some self-contained, in a quiet area near the casino and Pacific Fair shopping centre. A 20-minute but quite scenic walk to the beach. Good for children.

Other Accommodation

Other options include self-contained apartments, resorts, which offer a variety of ambiences and facilities, basic backpacker hostels and, for those who love the great outdoors, camping facilities and caravan sites.

Apartments are a common feature on the Gold Coast, where a two-room, fully self-contained unit, with equipped kitchen, laundry, television, telephone and a communal swimming pool, is available for $150–300 a day, although weekly rentals can be significantly cheaper.

Youth Hostel Association and other Hostels

Try www.backpackaround.com for comprehensive information.

Brisbane City YHA
392 Upper Roma Street, Brisbane 4000
Tel: 3236 1004
Fax: 3236 1947
www.yha.org.au
This modern hostel close to Brisbane Transit Centre includes a café and Internet kiosk. All rooms are air-conditioned; 20 of them sleep three or four; 28 are double/twin rooms; four are double/twin ensuite rooms. Well situated, especially if you want to enjoy Caxton Street's nightlife. $21–68.

Coolangatta/Kirra Beach YHA
230 Coolangatta Road, Bilinga
Queensland 4225
Tel: 5536 7644
Fax: 5599 5436
Next to Coolangatta airport. Tour bookings, surfboard hire, easy stroll to surf beaches. $15 (dormitory) to $44 family room.

The Palace Backpackers
Corner Ann and Edwards Streets
Brisbane 4000
Tel: 1800 676340
Fax: 3211 2466
www.palacebackpackers.com.au
Opposite central railway station. Basic lodgings close to cheap eateries. Plenty of noisy entertainment in the bar which stays open late. Good-value meals and rooftop sundeck. $20 for dormitory, $36 single, $48 double.

Backpacker Banana Bender
118 Petrie Terrace, Brisbane 4000
Tel: 3367 1157
Right in the middle of town, with a range of accommodation styles. Airport shuttle, Internet access and backpacker party nights.

HEALTH & EMERGENCIES

Hygiene and General Health

Public health regulation is comprehensive. Gastric problems from public eateries are rare and tap water is quite safe to drink.

Pharmacies

Sometimes called chemists. Plentiful and multi-functional, usually also stock camera film, cosmetics, toiletries and sometimes souvenirs. Many stay open late.

Medical/Dental Services

Standards are high. Unless you are from the UK, with which Australia has a reciprocal agreement, you will not be covered by the government's Medicare policy, so travel insurance is recommended. Without it, a visit to a doctor will cost you $35 and upwards. If admitted to a public hospital you'll pay $611

Above: one of Brisbane's helpful police officers

per day (minor treatment for outpatients is free) and an ambulance will cost $288 for the first 20km (12 miles), plus $9.65 for each additional kilometre. Dentists are expensive.

Crime/Trouble

Brisbane and rhe Gold Coast are both fairly safe, but don't leave valuables unattended or in parked cars. Avoid dark, empty spaces and public toilets at night. The police are helpful and competent. In an emergency, dial 000 for police, fire or ambulance.

COMMUNICATION & NEWS

Post

Post offices are open 9am–5pm, Mon–Fri; but the Brisbane GPO, 261 Queen St, City, is open 7am–7pm, Mon–Fri. Post offices will hold properly addressed mail for visitors.

Internet

Internet Cafés are plentiful and cheap:
Hub Communications, 125 Margaret St, Brisbane 4000
Tel: 3229 1119
www.thehub.com.au/cafe/
Java Bay, Bay St, Tweed Heads 2486
Tel: 5599 3232
Fax: 5599 3477
E-mail: info@javabay.com.au
www.javabay.com.au
Internet Express, 1st floor, Australia Fair Shopping Centre (in front of the Southport Cinemas)
E-mail: help@one.exp. com.au
www.exp.com.au/main/us.htm

Telephones

In the Australian telephone system (excluding mobiles), all six-figure numbers beginning with 13 are charged at the local-call rate of 25c from a private phone and 40c from a public pay phone. The same principle applies to all numbers that begin with 1300, followed by six digits. There is no charge for calls to phone numbers beginning with 1800. For ordinary eight-figure phone numbers, you need to use the 07 area code only if you're dialling from outside Queensland.

Room telephones are available in all but the cheapest accommodation, and most have switchboards compatible with modem communications, but you may need an adaptor, available at electronic shops.

The public and private telephone system is good; and most public phones take phone cards. Mobile-phone systems are compatible with everywhere but the Americas. If your provider offers a global roaming capability, you will find that you're in business as soon as you switch on.

Media

There's ample national and world coverage on hotel and apartment TV, and several large newsagents sell overseas newspapers, magazines and periodicals.

USEFUL INFORMATION

Disabled

A useful booklet, *Accessible Queensland*, and information on other disability support services, are available from the Disability Information Awareness Line (DIAL) weekdays on 3224 8444 in Brisbane, or toll-free outside Brisbane on 1800 177120.

Maps

These are accurate and readily available from concierges and information centres. *The Gold Coast Yellow Pages* contains some very good locality maps.

Right: keeping in touch

Language

Australia's language tends towards slightly modified English, which some humourists call 'Strine'. A book, *Let Stalk Strine*, which tried to codify the local parlance some years ago, focused on the extremes of the Australian drawl. Variations in accent tend to be along cultural rather than regional lines. Interpreter services can be obtained by phoning 131450. Charges may apply.

Sport

Sport is a major preoccupation of Australians, who engage in it with great vigour, debate and international success. It comes in numerous guises. There are four major football codes: rugby league, rugby union, soccer and Australian-rules football. While Australian-rules is traditionally the favourite among may dyed-in-the-wool locals, soccer is becoming more and more popular. Cricket, baseball, tennis, golf (there are more than 40 golf courses on the Gold Coast alone) and athletics all have large followings. Young visitors often go surf-mad.

It's easy to get information about forthcoming events from the Friday and weekend newspapers. The telephone directories' *Yellow Pages* contain a great deal of information on clubs and locations.

USEFUL ADDRESSES

Airlines and Agents

Aer Lingus, 217 George Street, Brisbane (tel: 3221 6479; www.aerlingus.com)
Air Caledonie, 217 George Street, Brisbane (tel: 3221 7272; www.air-caledonie.nc)
Air Nauru, 4-97 Creek Street, Brisbane (tel: 3229 6455; www.airnauru.com.au)
Air New Zealand, 133 Mary Street, Brisbane (tel: 132476; www.airnz.co.nz)
Air Niugini, 99 Creek Street, Brisbane (tel: 1300 361380; www.airniugini.com.pg)
Air Pacific, Level 4, 247 Adelaide Street, Brisbane (tel: 1800 230150; www.airpacific.com)
America West Airlines (tel: 1300 364757)
British Airways, Level 17, 241 Adelaide Street, Brisbane (tel: 3232 3000; www.britishairways.com)
Cathay Pacific, 400 Queen Street, Brisbane

(tel: 131747; www.cathaypacific.com)
Garuda Indonesia, 288 Edward Street, Brisbane (tel: 3210 0688; www.garuda-indonesia.com)
Gulf Air, 217 George Steet, Brisbane (tel: 3867 7188; www.gulfairco.com)
Japan Airlines, Level 14, Waterfront Place, 1 Eagle Street, Brisbane (tel: 3229 9922; www.jal.co.jp)
Korean Air, Ground floor, 400 Queen Street, Brisbane (tel: 3226 6000; www.koreanair.com)
Malaysian Airlines, Level 17, 80 Albert Street, Brisbane (tel: 3229 7117; www.malaysiaairlines.com.my)
Philippine Airlines, 141 Queen Street, Brisbane (tel: 3229 6022; www.philippineair.com)
Qantas Airways Ltd. (tel: 131313; www.qantas.com.au)
Royal Brunei, 25 Mary Street, Brisbane (tel: 3221 7757; www.bruneiair.com)
Singapore Airlines Ltd, 344 Queen Street, Brisbane (tel: 131011; www.singaporeair.com)
Sunstate Airlines (tel: 131313; www.qantas.com.au)
Thai Airways, 145 Eagle Street, Brisbane (tel: 3215 4700; www.thaiair.com)
United Airlines, 400 Queen Street, Brisbane (tel: 3221 7477; www.ual.com)
Virgin Blue, (tel: 136789; www.virginblue.com.au)

Above: one member of a sporting nation
Right: Tangalooma sunset

Hire Cars

Avis 1800 225533
Budget 132727
Hertz 133039
Roadsters convertibles 3252 3833
Thrifty 1300 367227.

Tourist Offices

Given Queensland's popularity amongst tourists, it's not surprising that the state is well-served by organisations designed to help visitors. In addition to information centres, the following organisations will answer almost any questions that you might have:

Queensland Tourism & Travel Corporation (tel: 3406 5343; fax: 3406 5564; www.qttc.com.au)

Tourism Brisbane (tel: 3221 8411; fax: 3229 5126)

Gold Coast (tel: 5592 2699; fax: 5570 3144)

National Parks

The parks listed below represent but a handful of the region's major national parks. For further information, call the Department of the Environment (tel: 3227 7111; www.env.qld.gov.au).

Lamington National Park tel: 5533 3584.

Mount Warning National Park tel: (02) 6672 6360.

Springbrook National Park (Natural Bridge) tel: 5533 5147.

Tamborine National Park tel: 5545 1171.

Moreton Island National Park tel: 3408 2710.

FURTHER READING

Insight Guide Australia, edited by Jeffery Pike, 2002. Background essays, a full rundown of attractions and practical advice, all supported by superb photography and full-colour maps.

The Wildlife of Greater Brisbane and *Wild Places of Greater Brisbane*, both Queensland Museum.

Moreton Bay People by Peter Ludlaw, self-published but in second printing.

Field Guide to the Birds of Australia by Graham Pizzey and Frank Knight, Angus & Robertson.

A Shorter History of Australia by Geoffrey Blainey, Random House, Australia.

The Explorers by Dr Tim Flannery, Penguin.

The Brisbane River: a Pictorial History by Robert Longhurst and William Douglas, W.D. Incorporated.

Changing Places Brisbane by Jan Jorgensen, Macmillan.

Captain James Cook: a Biography by Richard Hough, Coronet Books. The career of Australia's pre-eminent explorer.

Contemporary Aboriginal Art by Susan McCulloch, Allen & Unwin.

Heritage Trails of the Great South Coast, published by Queensland Environmental Protection Agency.

Take a Walk by John and Lyn Baly, Heron.

The Macquarie Dictionary, Macquarie University, Sydney. The definitive guide to Australian English.

ACKNOWLEDGEMENTS

Photography	**Steven Pohlner** *and*
Pages 10, 24, 35, 42, 66, 86	**Paul Phelan**
13 (both)	**The Courier Mail, Brisbane**
78	**QLD Tourist & Travel Corporation**
79	**Cable Ski World**
Cover, 8/9	**Jerry Dennis**
Back Cover	**Steven Pohlner**
Cover Design	**Carlotta Junger**
Production	**Tanvir Virdee**
Cartography	**Berndtson & Berndtson**

INDEX